That's Enterta

Steven Heller and

DESIGNED BY

Alexander Isley Design

inment

Anne Fink

PUBLISHED BY

PBC International, Inc.

Distributor to the book trade in the United States and Canada
Rizzoli International Publications Inc.
300 Park Avenue South
New York, NY 10010

Distributor to the art trade in the United States and Canada
PBC International, Inc.
One School Street
Glen Cove, NY 11542

Distributor throughout the rest of the world
Hearst Books International
1350 Avenue of the Americas
New York, NY 10019

Library of Congress Cataloging–in–Publication Data

Heller, Steven.
That's Entertainment : the graphics of showbiz /
Steven Heller, Anne Fink.
p.   cm.
Includes index.
ISBN 0-86636-344-0 (hb : alk. paper) —
ISBN 0-86636-480-3 (pb : alk. hb)
1. Performing arts   2. Graphic arts.   I. Fink, Anne.   II. Title.
PN1590.G73H45   1995   95-13985
741.6—dc20   CIP

CAVEAT— Information in this text is believed accurate, and
will pose no problem for the student or casual reader. However,
the author was often constrained by information contained in
signed release forms, information that could have been in error
or not included at all. Any misinformation (or lack of information)
is the result of failure in these attestations. The author has done
whatever is possible to insure accuracy.

Photography by Naum Kazhdan, 58 Third Street, Brooklyn,
New York 11218, unless otherwise noted.
Cover and introduction photography by Monica Stevenson.
Design by Alexander Isley Design

Color separation by Fine Arts Repro House Co., LTD., HK
Printing and binding by C&C Joint Printing Co., (H.K.) LTD., HK

Printed in Hong Kong

Contents

What's Entertainment?

*T*erms like visual communications or communication graphics not withstanding, a large proportion of graphic design *is* entertainment and the graphic designer is as much of an entertainer as any player on the stage, screen, or television. Although this may seem out of character for those designers who shy away from the public spotlight, graphic design is nevertheless another kind of mask behind which the visual entertainer performs. Regardless of subject, much of graphic design's type- and image-play is used for the purpose of attracting an audience's attention in order to impart information or message. To accomplish this goal there is no better way than by entertaining the viewer, reader, or passerby.

Graphic design has been closely allied with the entertainment industry in both supporting and primary roles. While a lot of graphic design is used to promote or advertise programs and events, a considerable amount of contemporary work transcends this fundamental requirement and is integral to the gestalt of an overall project. The best record sleeves, for example, are not merely containers but artworks that contribute to the recording artists' myth and image. Like the music itself, the imagery, typography, and complementary graphic components must appeal to an audience on a variety of levels. Graphic design cannot therefore be a neutral presence, it must inspire, beguile, and amuse—all synonyms for entertainment.

*G*raphic design did not, however, make an illustrious premiere. Entertainment advertising dating back to the early nineteenth century, when advancements in mass printing made the production of large bills and broadsides physically and economically feasible, was purely functional. During this period itinerant theater companies, as well as medicine shows, circuses and "legitimate" stage events were promoted through bills and posters that gave essential information with a minimum of embellishment. Usually set in bold woodblock letters they were devoid of extraneous decoration and rarely showed pictures of the performers. By the 1870s decorative elements were randomly included—job printers added stock printing cuts or clichés to the varied gothic and slab serif letterforms used to distinguish the names of the different acts. These bills were generally cluttered with diverse typographic material as a way to achieve greater visibility and grab viewer attention. Some were ad hoc but others were master pieces of exotic typographic composition. Yet it wasn't until the late nineteenth century, when chromolithography, or color printing, revolutionized the printing industry, that the poster became an integral art form as well as an advertising medium.

The most influential entertainment posters emanated from Parisian lithography shops during the 1890s and the most noteworthy were designed and illustrated by Henri Toulouse-Lautrec and Jules Cheret. Their brightly colored, impressionistic gestural representations of Moulin Rouge and Left Bank performers were the most visually exuberant imagery on the cluttered Parisian street hoardings. They were also visual icons of the *fin de siècle*. Lautrec, Cheret, and Czech born Alphonse Mucha, who designed posters promoting the great Sarah Bernhardt which are today paradigms of theatrical publicity, recast the role of graphics into both advertising and celebration. Posted throughout France they not only announced the season's great performances, they elevated the performers' image. In addition, they also catapulted the reputations of their creators. Owing to aesthetic innovations unique in the realms of fine and applied art these posters acquired lives of their own. Routinely torn off kiosks and hoardings, posters by these and lesser known *affichists* were sought after collectibles that transcended their ephemeral purpose as advertising art. Long after the promoted events closed, the posters continued to delight and entertain. Moreover, to this day these images provide a permanent visual record of the great and near great performances and performers.

By the early 1900s graphics for the burgeoning entertainment "industry" were among the most sophisticated forms of advertising art. Theater —drama, comedy, and musical—and later film were visual media that had to be promoted as such. Unlike most other advertising of the day for products and consumables, the image had to be more prominent than text. At the outset the conventions were minimal. Imagery was not governed by industry strictures (or egotistical demands) but by the graphic artist's imagination. The basic methodological principles concerned visibility—an image must be seen from at least 100 feet—and printing—the limitations of the press proscribed certain applications. But within such guidelines artist/designers had considerable freedom to interpret and embellish as they saw fit. The image could be wild or restrained as long as it was memorable. Yet predictably, as the entertainment industry matured so too did its promotional standards, and the graphics acquired a variety of conventions, clichés, and worse, a sense of self-importance.

*A*lthough theater graphics remained comparatively lively until the 1950s, at which point the genre suffered a two decade malaise brought about by excessive producer interference, it was around the 1920s that the problem of billing began to interfere with good design. Merely adding type to a pure image was not the real problem, rather the increasing number of stars, producers, and other vanity information altered the poster's appearance. Theater posters were soon governed by egos rather than aesthetics. Since this became the rule, the exception today are the comparatively few well-designed legitimate theater posters that do not subordinate image to billing. Yet the theater is not alone in allowing vanity to dominate. Nor was it the first to abandon the ostensibly pure image for typographic clutter.

When movie advertising started in earnest around the turn of the century, posters and lobby cards were a melange of image, title, blurb, and credits. By today's standards many of these are considered quaint, and indeed are good examples of how to pack a lot of information into a relatively small space and still maintain graphic appeal. But it established an unfortunate convention that has more or less plagued film posters to this day: too much visual junk. Nevertheless, the stylized, romantic realism of early-twentieth-century posters contributed to the movie mystique. Artwork at once depicted a paradigmatic scene while cele-brating its scene stealers. With a few notable exceptions in which sophisticated—sometimes abstract—graphic elements were used, most movie posters adhered to a kind of pulp novel man-nerism of visual exaggeration. Typographically they were the print equivalent of conventional movie trailers (or scenes of coming attractions); bold dimensional or shadowed title lettering screamed across the poster while collaged images offered a panoply of the movie's scenes.

Movie posters were urban carnival bills. They barked the merits of the acts and performances that they advertised. This method was so effective in attracting attention that it was also adopted as the principal model for advertising agencies to promote very different forms of entertainment. Take radio, for example: although radio per-formers were hidden from view, posters and press advertisements for this huge mass medium depicted the stars and characters of its programs in heroic portraits. Ironically, the advertising for this medium of mind left little to the imagination.

*A*fter mass media, more intimate shows including supper and nightclubs were the most prolifically advertised entertainments. In large American cities and small towns nightlife typified lifestyle. Nightclubs, the homes away from home for the gadfly set, housed big and small bands, singers and chanteuses, jokesters and magicians—all of which required promotion. In the 1930s Art Moderne, or Art Deco, was the principle style and graphic "dress" that the swankier of these nightspots put on. The equivalent of today's hip and chic rock clubs and discos, Jazz age nightclubs were promoted as the places to be and be seen. Their owners plastered their environs with posters, bills, and programs which were masterpieces of stylized expression every bit as raucous in their day as grunge rave cards are now.

*T*he beginning of another important legacy of entertainment graphics began in 1939 when for the first time art adorned a record sleeve. Recordings were initially promoted through artfully created point-of-purchase displays and in-shop, counter posters which sat in close proximity to the product; but the albums themselves were little but drab craftpaper wrappers over boards. Although the earliest album covers merely reprinted existing paintings, mini-poster covers exclusively designed for the purpose of selling music made an immediate impact on the market. The first breakthrough was Alex Steinweiss's covers for Columbia Records. They were eye-catching, symbolic interpretations of jazz, classical, and popular music designed in the manner of the Modern European advertising posters. They were also the first covers to include type and image that at once gave an identity to the music or recording artist and also to the record company itself. The discovery that record art encouraged increased sales prompted other major labels to introduce graphics. So within only a few years of its introduction album art became a vital marketing and packaging tool.

*B*efore record albums adopted art, Modern graphic design was only incidentally applied to entertainment graphics. In fact, Modern graphic design was in its nascent developmental stage until after World War II when the designers who had been influenced by the Bauhaus and other European Modern movements were encouraged to apply their theories of graphic functionalism to a variety of new institutional and corporate media. Although most mass advertising continued to be mired in the hard-sell conventions in place before the war, certain aspects were nevertheless transformed by those iconoclasts using the Modern idioms. One such pioneer was Saul Bass, who revolutionized movie advertising by introducing abstract symbols to a genre where hyperrealist vignettes were convention. He further reduced the amount of vanity and selling copy in a medium where more was better than less. That was just in print. He also applied these ideas to the silver screen with his reinvention of movie titles.

Executed by editors in movie optical houses, title sequences were never touched by graphic designers, and rarely considered an integral. Bass, however, intuited that this opening sequence could both show the title and credits as well as introduce the story or plot. In *Man with a Golden Arm* the expressionistic graphic used as the film's print logo was animated in such a way that it became a preface to the story. In subsequent titles he combined graphics with live action to symbolically establish an identity for the film and begin the storytelling process. Bass influenced others to develop content-based titles, notably Steven Frankfurt who created a riveting title sequence for *To Kill A Mocking Bird*. Today Richard Greenberg is the master of this form for having both produced engaging film openers and inventing the technology needed to make them happen. His most famous include openings for *Superman*, in which the comic book page comes to life, and *The World According To Garp*, where a baby slowly bounces against the clouds. Although these rely less on pure graphics than Bass's titles, they are decidedly influenced by page design and are graphically composed.

Entertainment graphics reached another plateau in the late 1960s when the volcano of youth culture that spewed rock and roll into the air released a lava flow of progressive graphics. The psychedelic posters, a melange of retrofitted imagery and souped-up lettering set against a background of vibrating, fluorescent color were as resolutely entertaining as the concerts they advertised. Like the posters of Lautrec, Cheret, and Mucha, these youth culture icons were torn off lampposts and sold in headshops to an audience who took as much pleasure from their visual exuberance as they did in the happenings in the nation's rock palaces. The original psychedelic posters by San Francisco artists Victor Moscoso, Wes Wilson, Rick Griffin, and Mouse and Kelley, spawned a huge following of imitators, which further launched a graphics revolution that forever altered the way graphic design was applied to entertainment promotion and publicity.

Subsequent graphic movements, including '70s Punk, '80s New Wave, and '90s Grunge were all built upon the foundation laid down during the late '60s by the psychedelicists. Even graphics created by comparatively mainstream designers for such hot entertainment industries as record companies adopted many of the graphic characteristics (and tics) of the psychedelicists. The master of Modernism, Ivan Chermayeff (Chermayeff & Geismar) developed a vibrating typeface in the late '60s used in advertisements for New York's East Village rock club, The Electric Circus.

Entertainment graphics cannot be pigeonholed according to any definitive style. As the psychedelicists turned up the visual volume, other designers for mainstream entertainments continued to modulate between classic and late Modern approaches. By the '70s, when the number of graphic designers began to surge higher, however, entertainment industries became a focal point for more experimental approaches. The music industry, of course, has always encouraged the unconventional. Indeed it could be argued the Lautrecs and Cherets of the late twentieth century are mini-poster record sleeve designers. Of course, with the advent of compact disks forcing the extinction of LPs, graphics in this medium have markedly changed to accommodate the smaller size making miniaturists out of posterists. So during the '70s and '80s the real latter-day Lautrecs and Cherets were still those who worked in the poster medium. And the industries that use posters most are the traditional ones—theater, film, and more and more, television.

The most eye-catching, if not memorable, entertainment graphics of this era are Paul Davis's posters for New York's Public Theater and James McMullan's posters for Lincoln Center's Vivian Beaumont Theater. Both recapture the golden age of the *fin de siècle* when image and art triumphed over vanity copy. There was not a word about the stars or the director; even the favorable critical blurbs were left for the press advertisements. Only image and a simple integrated, hand-lettered title by the artists themselves identified these masterpieces of tradition and contemporaneity. While Davis and McMullan reinvigorated the theatrical poster,

Chemayeff & Geismar, Milton Glaser, Seymour Chwast and other leading American *affichists* inaugurated an entirely new genre—the bus shelter poster, primarily advertising subsidized programs on Public Television. A new vehicle for advertising, an illuminated display, was born with the introduction of bus shelters in the late '70s. Outdoor advertising companies were quick to exploit its potential; Mobil and Texaco oil companies, sponsors of Masterpiece Theater and Great Performances respectively, were among the earliest users. It was their need to promote programming that encouraged a widespread entertainment poster renaissance which continues to this day.

The bus shelter has also given rise to a slew of poster alternatives. And depending on geographical location, the posters for theater companies, concerts, and other mainstream and alternative entertainments run the graphic design gamut from radically experimental to devoutly traditional. In fact, this is how to best characterize the period surveyed in this book. For the entertainment graphics of the '90s is an eclectic, often raucous mix. The work selected for this volume and organized into four key categories—theater, film, music and television—includes a variety of personal and period styles as well as a range of typographic, photographic, illustrative, and even digital manifestations.

To understand the reason for making this compilation we must reprise the beginning of this introduction. Graphic design is in large part entertainment and entertainment graphics are in large part the most exciting aspect of graphic design. Exceptions resulting from vanity and ego to the contrary, this is one of the most fertile areas for experimentation (and sometimes indulgence), and what emerges are often paradigms for designers in other realms. Entertainment graphics are windows on the cultural scene. The work by scores of contemporary (veteran and neophyte) designers found in this volume document a distinct period of graphic and artistic innovation. While some of the material is as ephemeral as the performance it promotes, others will no doubt define the graphic milieu for decades to come. But the criteria for inclusion here is not based on any long-term prediction of greatness, but rather whether in the time in which the work is produced it succeeds both in promoting and entertaining.

Theater

*G*raphic design evolved from a muddle of Victorian era slab serif typography, which typified early theatrical posters, into a muddle of post-modern typographic layering, which characterizes what has been alternately referred to as New Wave, Deconstruction, and Grunge. Along the way, various permutations and numerous styles have defined the ephemeral character of graphic design. The theater poster has played a pivotal role in this evolutionary process, for graphic design arguably grew out of the earliest theater bills, notices, and announcements produced by job printers. The first "designed" pieces, late-nineteenth-century "art" posters, advertised all manner of theatrical events and set standards that continue to this day.

*B*ut graphics promoting theatrical productions have radically changed since the poster's golden age during the fin de siècle. Legitimate theater forced conventions that have constricted how the poster looks. A walk down Shubert Alley in the heart of New York's theater district supports the fact that poster graphics are the least important aspect of a show's promotion.

Blurb-ridden, star-studded newspaper and television ads are the most strategically important—and "art" posters are relegated to secondary status. But most of the posters drown under the typographic weight of press plaudits and star billing where the central image appears as almost an afterthought. Yet there are notable exceptions.

Iconic posters for New York's Public Theater, originally created by Paul Davis in the 1970s and '80s and currently designed by Paula Scher of Pentagram, recall both the nascent period of theatrical advertising and the golden age of poster design. Davis revived the fin de siècle's *painterly poster tradition*, while Scher reapplies the Victorian penchant for mixing various sizes of gothics and serifs. Like Davis, James McMullan's current posters for Lincoln Center's Viviene Beaumont Theater are painterly and gestural, and so spiritually recall a bygone era of early graphic design. This work generally transcends the generic theater poster because it consciously reveals the personalities of its makers—these are not anonymous or generic signs. Yet these posters are nevertheless exceptions to the rule for the legitimate theater.

*M*ost posters doggedly follow the conventions described above. So in a sea of mediocre graphic design, the most eye-catching graphics are the quirkier and often the least glittery posters, flyers, and brochures created for off-Broadway and alternative theater groups. These are not the 24-sheet billboards that hang in Times Square or "one-sheets" posted in suburban railroad stations, but the cheaply printed, illegally hung announcements that obliterate the "post no bills" signs on most scaffolds and hoardings. Raucous graphic design for off-off-Broadway, counter-culture and alternative live performances is no more qualitatively consistent than for the mammoth-budget shows, but as a rule it exhibits more variety and takes greater risks. In a genre where entertainment graphics are often not as bold—or entertaining—as what they advertise, alternative graphics experiment as they entertain.

Poster
Tiny Alice

Client
Fells Point Corner Theatre

Designer/Typographer
Paul Sahre

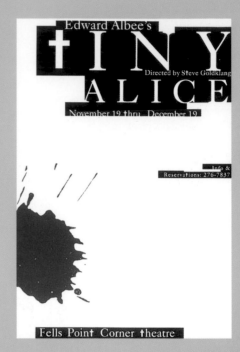

Poster
Love and Anger

Client
Fells Point Corner Theatre

Designer/Typographer
Paul Sahre

Poster
A Lie of the Mind

Client
Fells Point Corner Theatre

Designers
**Paul Sahre
David Plunkert**

Typographer
Paul Sahre

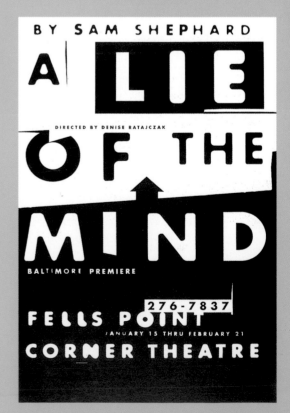

RICHARD III

Theater
19

Poster
Richard III

Client
**The Shakespeare
Project**

Firm
Victore Design Works

Art Director/Designer/
Illustrator/Photographer
James Victore

Bill T. Jones and Arnie Zane Dance Company

Bill T. Jones/Arnie Zane & Company

Mershon Auditorium

February 15

8:00 p.m.

$18, $14, $12, $10

Program:
The Last Supper at Uncle Tom's Cabin

Since the death from AIDS of his collaborator and life partner, Arnie Zane, dancer/choreographer Bill T. Jones has been an impassioned artist, searching for the meaning of Zane's death and his own mortality. In *The Last Supper at Uncle Tom's Cabin*, Jones explores these and other social and political issues, creating a work that promises to be one of the season's most memorable and controversial events.

Bill T. Jones and Arnie Zane formed a full-time company after 11 years of working together as a duo. With eloquent, sculptural tableaux, intensely dramatic gestures and awe-inspiring virtuosic feats, the company zoomed onto the international dance scene in the early 1980s. Jones and Zane, a study in physical contrasts as well as movement styles, were noted for their innovative use of partnering, body juxtaposition and dynamic technique.

Jones' collaborators have included the legendary drummer Max Roach, the late graffiti artist Keith Haring and the late fashion designer Willi Smith.

The current company of 10 dancers has appeared in 25 states and 22 countries, performing to nearly 55,000 people annually.

Sankai Juku

Sankai Juku

Mershon Auditorium

November 10

8:00 p.m.

$22, $18, $14, $10

Program: *Unetsu (The Egg Stands Out of Curiosity)*

The stage is dominated by a pool of water. Two dancers, dance in the water, Christ-like figures, whose slowly flowing movements of limbs fall under. Carefully egg-shaped sheets are suspended of about the pool.

In the simplest way, full descent from the Mershon stage will soon, when Juku's forward, turns composer brings its mysterious, spellbinding dance theater to Columbus. Under the artistic direction of Ushio Amagatsu, Sankai Juku has fascinated Western audiences since 1980 when it first performed in Europe. In 1984, the company made its North American debut at the Toronto International Festival and the Los Angeles Olympic Arts Festival. Since then Sankai Juku has performed extensively throughout the United States, earning critics and audiences.

Butoh, a new Japanese art form evolved during the 1960s as an expression of humanitarian awareness by that country's post-war generations. Followers of Butoh rejected the traditional forms in Eastern and Western dances. They investigated a method of expression which could reflect the body and feeling of their generation. The Amagatsu, Butoh expresses the language of the body rather than a theoretical inventory of movement.

The name Sankai Juku can be translated to mean "studio from the land of mountains and sea."

photographer: Philip Martin

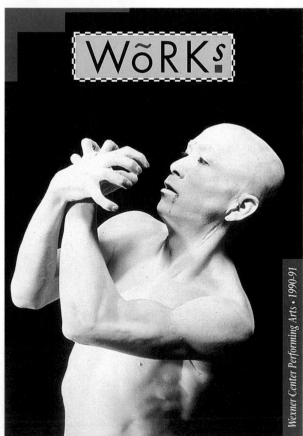

Brochure
Works 1990-91

Client/Firm
Wexner Center for the Arts/The Ohio State University

Designers
Alan Jazak
Rich Rinsma

Photographers
Philip Martin (above)
Herbert Migdoli (right)

WõRKs

Wexner Center Performing Arts • 1990-91

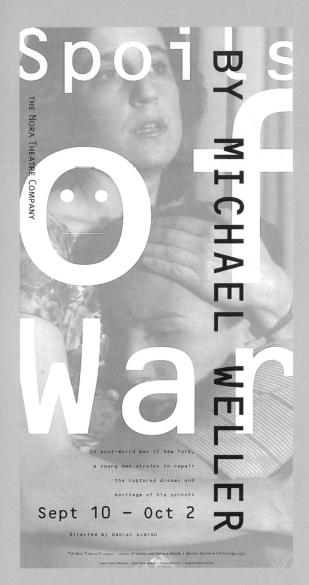

Poster
Spoils of War

Client
Nora Theatre

Firm
Fahrenheit

Designers/Typographers
Paul Montie
Carolyn Montie

Photographer
Kippy Goldfarb

Poster
Nureyev at Lehman Center

Client
Lehman Center for the Arts

Art Direction
Grey Advertising

Firm
Schumaker

Designer/Illustrator/
Calligrapher
Ward Schumaker

Poster
Blade to the Heat

Client
The Public Theater

Firm
Pentagram Design

Art Director
Paula Scher

Designers
Paula Scher
Ron Louie
Lisa Mazur

Poster
Him

Client
The Public Theater

Firm
Pentagram Design

Art Director
Paula Scher

Designers
Paula Scher
Ron Louie
Lisa Mazur

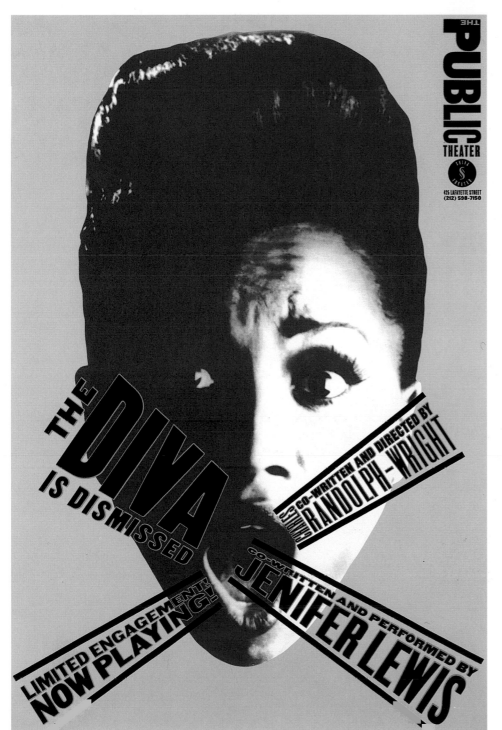

Poster
The Public Theater

Client
The Public Theater

Firm
Pentagram Design

Designers
Paula Scher
Ron Louie
Lisa Mazur

Photography
Pentagram Design

Poster
The Diva Is Dismissed

Client
The Public Theater

Firm
Pentagram Design

Art Director
Paula Scher

Designers
Paula Scher
Ron Louie
Lisa Mazur

Photographer
Teresa Lizotte

Poster
Gray's Anatomy

Client
ACT Theatre

Firm
Modern Dog

Art Directors
Michael Strassburger
Teri Mumme

Designer/Illustrator/
Typographer
Michael Strassburger

Poster
The Velveteen Rabbit, Ballet

Client
The Oberlin Dance Collective

Firms
The Graphic Eye
Schumaker

Art Director
Sue Ehnebuske

Designer/Illustrator/
Calligrapher
Ward Schumaker

Poster
Tossing and Turning

Client
Pickle Family Circus

Firm
Michael Mabry Design

Art Director/Designer/
Illustrator/Photographer
Michael Mabry

Pin
**SUNY Purchase
Performing Arts**

Firm
Drenttel Doyle Partners

Designer
Tom Kluepfel

Illustrator
Steven Guarnaccia

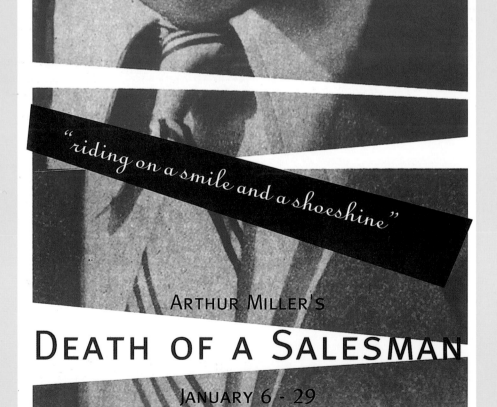

THE NORA THEATRE COMPANY

"riding on a smile and a shoeshine"

ARTHUR MILLER'S

DEATH OF A SALESMAN

JANUARY 6 - 29

Directed by Eric Engel

The Nora Theatre Company • corner of Quincy and Harvard Streets • Harvard Square • call 617/495-4530
Latecomers cannot be admitted

graphic design: Fahrenheit • printing: Wizgald Press • pre-press: Graphics Express

Poster
Death of a Salesman

Client
Nora Theatre

Firm
Fahrenheit

Designers/Typographers
Paul Montie
Carolyn Montie

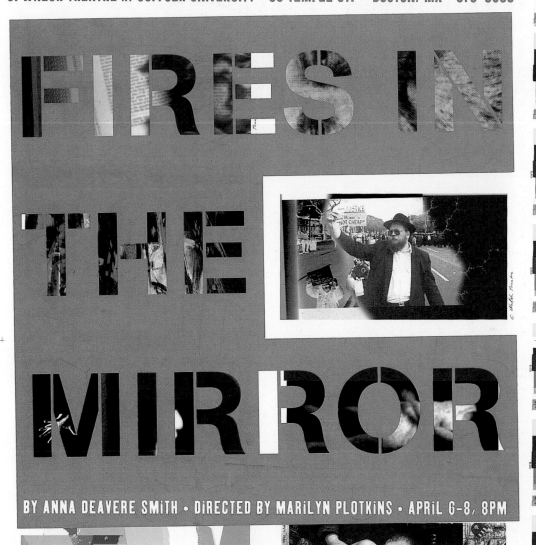

C. WALSH THEATRE AT SUFFOLK UNiVERSiTY • 55 TEMPLE ST. • BOSTON, MA • 573-8680

FIRES IN THE MIRROR

BY ANNA DEAVERE SMiTH • DiRECTED BY MARiLYN PLOTKiNS • APRiL 6-8, 8PM

Poster
Fires in the Mirror

Client
C. Walsh Theatre

Firm
Fahrenheit

Art Director/Designer
Paul Montie

Photographer
Andy Uzzie

Postcards
C. Walsh Theatre

Client
C. Walsh Theatre

Firm
Fahrenheit

Art Director/Designer/
Illustrator
Paul Montie

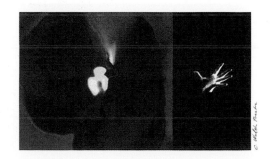

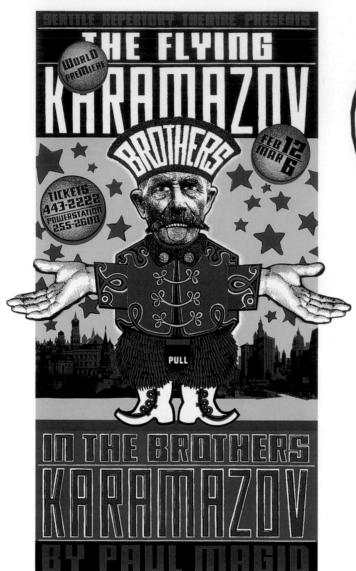

Logo
Circus Flora

Client
Circus Arts Foundation

Firm
Phoenix Creative

Designer/Illustrator/
Hand Letterer
Ed Mantels-Seeker

Poster
**The Flying Karamazov
Brothers**

Client
**Seattle Repertory
Theatre**

Firm
Modern Dog

Art Directors
**Vittorio Costarella
Robynne Raye
Michael Strassburger**

Designer/Illustrator/
Typographer
Vittorio Costarella

Poster
Beach Blanket Babylon

Client
Club Fugazi

Art Director
Steve Silver

Firms
**Michael Schwab Design
Beach Blanket Babylon**

Designer/Illustrator
Michael Schwab

Typographer
Andresen Typographics

Poster
**Alice B. Theatre 1991-92
Season**

Client
Alice B. Theatre

Firm
Modern Dog

Art Director
Rick Rankin

Designers
Michael Strassburger
Robynne Raye

Illustrator
Vittorio Costarella

Typographer
Robynne Raye

Poster
The Substance of Fire

Client
Seattle Repertory Theatre

Firm
Modern Dog

Art Directors
Robynne Raye
Doug Hughes

Designer/Typographer
Robynne Raye

SEATTLE REPERTORY THEATRE PRESENTS

THE SUBSTANCE OF FIRE

BY JON ROBIN BAITZ

OCTOBER 28 - NOVEMBER 15
ON STAGE 2 • TICKETS 443.2222

Poster Printed on recycled paper by The

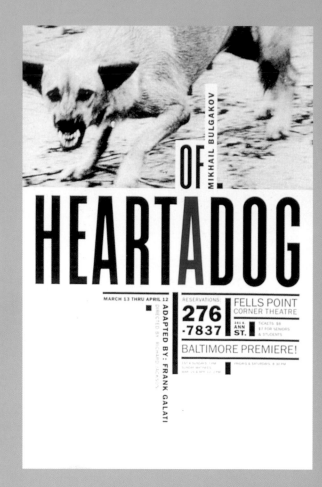

MIKHAIL BULGAKOV

OF HEARTADOG

MARCH 13 THRU APRIL 12

RESERVATIONS:
276 -7837

FELLS POINT
CORNER THEATRE

TICKETS: $8
$7 FOR SENIORS
& STUDENTS

BALTIMORE PREMIERE!

ADAPTED BY: FRANK GALATI

Poster
Heart of a Dog

Client
Fells Point Corner Theatre

Designers
Paul Sahre
Gregg Heard

Photographer
Lew Bush

Typographer
Paul Sahre

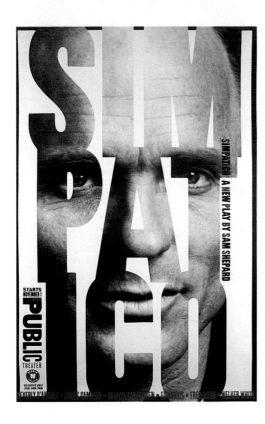

Poster
Simpatico

Client
The Public Theater

Firm
Pentagram Design

Art Director
Paula Scher

Designers
Paula Scher
Ron Louie
Lisa Mazur

Poster
Some People

Client
The Public Theater

Firm
Pentagram Design

Art Director
Paula Scher

Designers
Paula Scher
Ron Louie
Lisa Mazur

Photographer
Paula Court

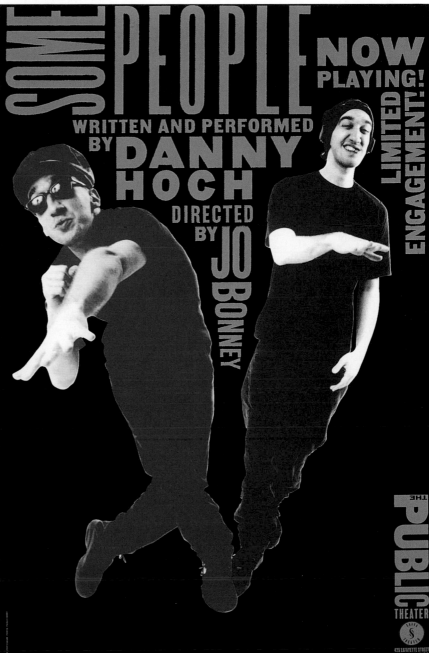

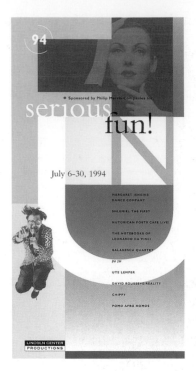

For '94, Serious Fun! is highlighting the works of artists celebrated for blazing new trails. We've got multi-media events — major new works, original musical theater presentations, New York Premieres, unique collaborations. This year's Serious Fun! is more diverse than ever — it's performance in a big way. • So big, that we've added a new performance space — the John Jay Theatre. Located just a few blocks from Lincoln Center, John Jay is an intimate environment that adds a new dimension to our offerings. • Serious Fun! '94 runs the gamut from hip to hip-hop. It covers everything from West Texas to Avenue A. Serious Fun! has a reputation for launching new works by bold artists like Karen Finley, Bill Irwin and David Shiner, Blue Man Group and Eric Bogosian. This year, it's the place to witness the worlds of dance and poetry converge (The Gates by Margaret Jenkins Dance Company), watch jazz and video fuse (Max Roach, Kit Fitzgerald & Donald Byrd in JU JU), see realities explode (David Rousseve's Pop Dreams), hear poetry hit the wall (Nuyorican Poets Cafe Live!), experience klezmer as you've never heard it before (Shlemiel The First) and even discover a country & western musical (Chippy). • Serious Fun! promises to be one of the hottest tickets of the long hot summer. So book early and join the Fun!

Nuyorican Poets Cafe Live!

ALICE TULLY HALL

Saturday **July 9** 7:30pm

"...A BOHEMIAN RHAPSODY OF RAP SWAGGER AND FIERCELY URBAN POEMS..."
NEWSWEEK

"...A SELF-CONSCIOUSLY OUTRAGEOUS MULTICULTURAL VARIETY SHOW."
NEW YORK OBSERVER

Think poetry is something you just read in books? This group of power poets will change your mind forever. These are the artists who are responsible for the resurgence of poetry that's appearing everywhere these days — from the cover of New York Magazine to GAP ads. Fresh from the Nuyorican Poets' Cafe on Manhattan's Lower East Side, these poets use words like weapons. In their hands, a metaphor is an instrument of deadly destruction — or deconstruction. Theirs is poetry with an attitude, an edge. This is definitely not the stuff of freshman English. It's performance. It's parody. It's rap. It's dance. And its inspirations come from strange and unexpected places — the Jetsons, MTV, Bill Clinton, Joey Buttafuoco, Avenue A. In fact, this poetry is so muscular, these poets don't have readings, they have slams.

The Notebooks of Leonardo Da Vinci

Fresh from its sensational sold-out run at Chicago's Goodman Theatre, The Notebooks of Leonardo Da Vinci is a visually riveting theatrical production based on the notebooks of Renaissance genius Leonardo Da Vinci. An intriguing "dream document" fashioned out of layer upon layer of stage visuals, acrobatic moves and spoken words, Leonardo takes us on a voyage through the mind of one of the world's great thinkers. Da Vinci's musings on motion, light, perspective and anatomy come to life on stage as the ensemble cast swing through the air, balance, manipulate ropes and strike poses. The result: a rare and brilliant psychological landscape alternately humorous, witty and illuminating.

Leonardo is a triumphant celebration of human passion, imagination and intelligence.

Adapted and directed by Mary Zimmerman. Performed by members of the original Goodman Theatre production. Music by Michael Bodeen and Miriam Sturm. Sets designed by Scott Bradley. Costumes by Allison Reeds. Lighting by T.J. Gerckens.

JOHN JAY THEATRE

Wed **July 13** 8pm
Thurs **July 14** 8pm
Fri **July 15** 8pm
Sat **July 16** 8pm

"AN INDISPUTABLE MASTERPIECE IN BOTH CONCEPT AND REALIZATION... HAUNTING, BRILLIANT AND PHENOMENALLY BEAUTIFUL"
CHICAGO SUN-TIMES

Brochure
Serious Fun!

Client/Firm
Lincoln Center for the Performing Arts, Inc.

Art Director
Susan Panetta

Designer
Eric Van Den Brulle

For Season Schedule Call:
623-5510

UNCENSORED
UNCUT
UNEXPECTED
...

THE PERFORMANCE PLACE · 277 BROADWAY SOMERVILLE

Photo: The Devil's Chauffeur

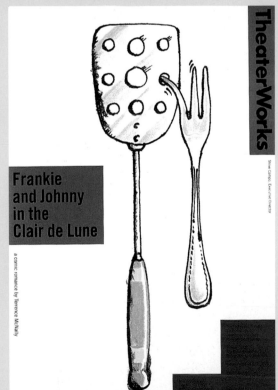

TheaterWorks

Steve Campo, Executive Director

Frankie
and Johnny
in the
Clair de Lune

a comic romance by Terrence McNally

Poster
**Uncensored, Uncut,
Unexpected**

Client
The Performance Place

Firm
Fahrenheit

Designers/Typographers
**Paul Montie
Carolyn Montie**

Photographer
The Devil's Chauffeur

Poster
**Frankie and Johnny in the
Clair de Lune**

Client
TheaterWorks

Firm
Peter Good Graphic Design

Art Director/Designer/
Illustrator/Typographer
Peter Good

Poster
K-2

Client
TheaterWorks

Firm
Peter Good Graphic Design

Art Director/Designer/
Illustrator/Typographer
Peter Good

Photographer
Jim Coon

Poster
Jacob's Pillow 1990

Client
Jacob's Pillow

Firm
Chermayeff & Geismar Inc.

Design Director/Designer/
Illustrator
Ivan Chermayeff

Invitation
Dance with the Dancers

Client
New York City Ballet

Firm
Sagmeister Inc.

Art Director/Designer/
Illustrator/Typographer
Stefan Sagmeister

Poster
**SUNY Purchase
Performing Arts
Center**

Firm
**Drenttel Doyle
Partners**

Designer
Tom Kluepfel

Illustrator
Steven Guarnaccia

Rule 1: Never do it without a rubber. If he's got a "Johnny" on you've less chance of picking something up.Rule 2: If you do get something — I've had NSU and I get cystitis all the time — have it checked right away at the nearest clap clinic. They'll always treat your case in total confidence.Rule 3: If they do turn nasty — and they do — never show you're frightened. Stand your ground, raise your voice. If they think they're going to be part of a scene they'll lose their nerve and scarper.Rule 4: Try and get all the money off him at the start. This way if he's huffing and puffing and getting nowhere you can always tell him time's up and he's had his chips.Rule 5: Set a time limit — twenty minutes at the most, and never go over it unless they're paying extra, obviously.Rule 6: Avoid picking up in places known to the police. I work the bowling alley, local library, even the local Conservative Club. I do less business but although I've had a couple of warnings I've never been busted.Rule 7: Never drink on the job. Keep your wits about you. If there's something about him you don't like, steer clear. Life's too short, why take risks? Rule 8: If you have to go with somebody you haven't sussed out, never take him back — try and do it somewhere where there's people not too far away and there's plenty of light. Similarly never get into a car.Rule 9: I'll only do straight sex or hand jobs. I've never done oral or Greek, but I suppose it's up to you to decide what you'll do.Rule 10: Don't get too greedy. More than three or four a night and your judgement starts going. Know when to call it a night.

A gritty depiction of three women's determined struggle to resist the tides of economic despair.

THATCHER'S
WOMEN

A play by **Kay Adshead**, directed by Judy Braha
May 6 – 29 Call 617/495-4530

The Nora Theatre Company · corner of Quincy and Harvard Streets in Harvard Square

Poster
Angels in America

Client
**Theater Communications
Group**

Firm
Milton Glaser Inc.

Art Director/Designer/
Illustrator
Milton Glaser

Poster
Thatcher's Women

Client
Nora Theatre

Firm
Fahrenheit

Designers/Typographers
**Paul Montie
Carolyn Montie**

Poster
Carousel

Client
Lincoln Center Theater

Firms
James McMullan Inc.
Russek Advertising

Art Director
Jim Russek

Designer/Illustrator
James McMullan

Poster
Ghosts Play One

Client
**Fells Point Corner
Theatre**

Designer/Typographer
Paul Sahre

Poster
**Baby with the
Bathwater**

Client
**Fells Point Corner
Theatre**

Designers
**Paul Sahre
David Plunkert**

Typographer
Paul Sahre

closer than ever

Fells Point Corner Theatre

January 17 thru February 16

Music by: David Shire

Baltimore Premiere!

Lyrics by: Richard Maltby, Jr.

Musical Direction by: Tim Delaney

251 South Ann Street
Tickets: $10
$8 for seniors and students
Fridays and Saturdays: 8:30pm
First four Sundays: 7pm
Sunday matinees Feb. 2 and
Feb. 16: 2pm

For more information call: 276-7837

Directed by: Terry J. Long

Poster
Closer Than Ever

Client
**Fells Point Corner
Theatre**

Designers/Illustrators
**Paul Sahre
Chris Panzer**

Typographer
Paul Sahre

The Nora Theatre Company
P.O. Box 2764
Cambridge, MA 02238
(617) 495-4530

Non-Profit
Organization
US Postage
PAID
Boston, MA
Permit #
57114

Roberta Willison

gold containing a large percentage of silver. [L., < Gr.*elektron*
amber.]
e-lec´tu-a-ry, 1 ɪ-lek´´chu-[*or* -tiu-]ē-ri;   2 e-lĕc´´chu-[*or* -tū-]ā
ry, *n.* [-RIES², *pl.*] A confection made by incorporating a medicin
with some sweet substance. [< LL. *electuarium,* < Gr. *ekleikton*
< *ek,* out,+ *leicho* , lick.]

el´´e-e-mos´y-na-ry, ĕl´´e-e-mŏs´y-nā-ry. *adj.* **1.** Of, relating to, o
contributed as charity. [< Gr. *eleēmosynē;* see ALMS.] **2.** A pla
by *Lee Blessing* in which three generations of women are boun
together by the love and dreams they share. *Presented by*
[TheaterWorks] at the Bronson & Hutensky Theater – 233 Pear
Street, Downtown Hartford. January 11 through February 10
1991. Performances Wednesdays through Saturdays at 8 p.m
and Sunday matinees at 2:30 p.m. *Tickets* $10; college student
& seniors $8; high school students – free. For tickets *call* 527
7838. *Presented* with the cooperation of the Hartford Advocat
and made possible by United Technologies Corporation
el´e´-gant, 1 el´ɪ-gant; 2 ĕl´e-ḡant, *a.* **1.** Marked by refine
ment, grace, or symmetry; as of action, form or structure; als
possessing or exhibiting refined taste. **2.** Possessing a fine sens

Poster
Eleemosynary

Client
TheaterWorks

Firm
**Peter Good Graphic
Design**

Art Director/Designer/
Typographer
Peter Good

Mailer
1993-94 Season Schedule

Client
Nora Theatre

Firm
Fahrenheit

Designers/Typographers
Paul Montie
Carolyn Montie

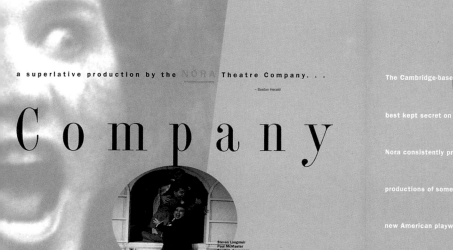

a superlative production by the NORA Theatre Company. . .
— Boston Herald

Company

The Cambridge-based **NORA** Theatre Company is the

best kept secret on the Boston theater scene...

Nora consistently provides solid and imaginative

productions of some of the best work by

new American playwrights. — Bay Windows

Steven Longmuir
Paul McMaster

Steven Longmuir
Photo: Eric Levens

[THE AMERICAN PREMIERE!]
RESERVATIONS: 276-7837
MAP OF THE HEART
BY: WILLIAM NICHOLSON
DIRECTOR: ROBERT CLINGAN
$9/$8 FOR SENIORS AND STUDENTS
NOVEMBER 13 - DECEMBER 20
FELLS POINT CORNER THEATRE
251 SOUTH ANN STREET

Poster
Map of the Heart

Client
Fells Point Corner
Theatre

Designers
Paul Sahre
David Plunkert
Joe Parisi

Illustrators
David Plunkert
Paul Sahre

Typographer
Paul Sahre

Poster
Bay Street 1993

Client
**Bay Street Theatre
Festival**

Firm
Paul Davis Studio

Art Director/Designer/
Illustrator
Paul Davis

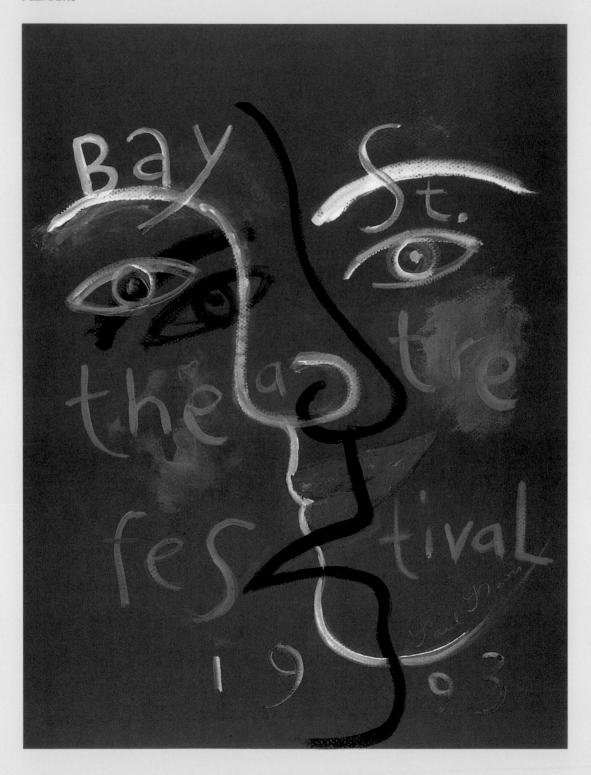

Poster
Richard III

Client
**New York Shakespeare
Festival**

Firm
Paul Davis Studio

Art Director/Designer/
Illustrator
Paul Davis

Postcard
Invisible Cities

Client
Invisible Cities Group

Firm
Fahrenheit

Designers/Typographers
**Paul Montie
Carolyn Montie**

Photographer
Gary Duehr

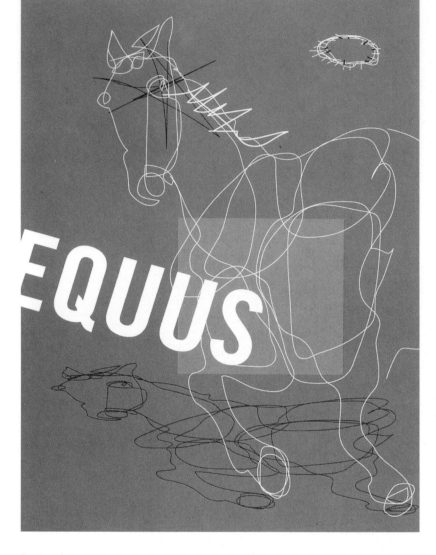

Poster
Scotland Road

Client
TheaterWorks

Firm
Peter Good Graphic Design

Art Director/Designer/
Illustrator/Typographer
Peter Good

Photographer
Jim Coon

Postcard
Equus

Client
C. Walsh Theatre

Firm
Fahrenheit

Designers/Typographers
Paul Montie
Carolyn Montie

Illustrator
Paul Montie

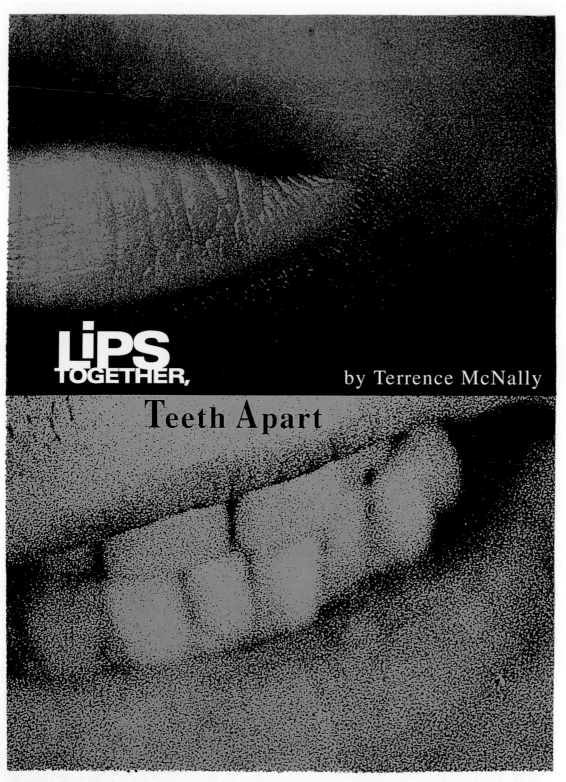

LIPS
TOGETHER,

by Terrence McNally

Teeth Apart

Seattle Repertory Theatre • Jan. 6 - 30 • Tickets 443.2222 PowerStation 255.2600

Poster by Modern Dog. Printing by Two Dimensions with water-based inks on recycled paper.

Poster
Lips Together, Teeth Apart

Client
Seattle Repertory Theatre

Firm
Modern Dog

Designer/Typographer
Robynne Raye

Theater
45

Poster
**50 Beautiful Improvisions
& 3 Ugly Ones**

Client
Unexpected Theatre

Designer
Art Chantry

Logo
Two Trains Running

Client
The Old Globe Theater

Firm
Visual Asylum

Designer
MaeLin Levine

Illustrator
David Jervis

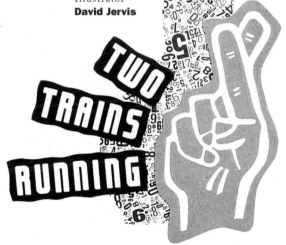

Logo
La Fiaca

Client
The Old Globe Theater

Firm
Visual Asylum

Designer/Illustrator
Amy Levine

Poster
Images Teen Theater

Client
Planned Parenthood

Firm
Visual Asylum

Designer
Amy Levine

Photographer
Eric Tucker

Poster
Alley Apples

Client
Fells Point Corner Theatre

Designer/Typographer
Paul Sahre

Theater
48

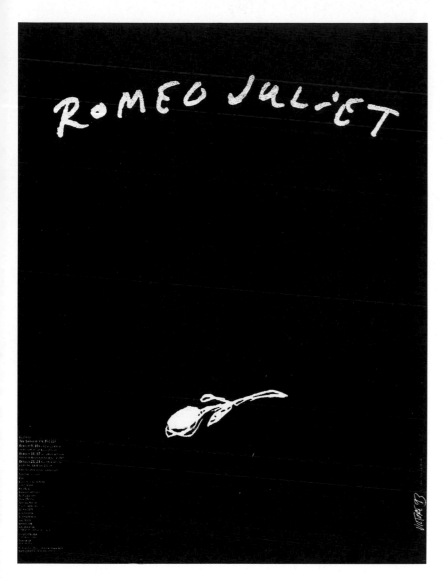

Poster
Romeo Juliet

Client
**The Shakespeare
Project**

Firm
Victore Design Works

Art Director/Designer
Illustrator/Typographer
James Victore

Poster
**Italian American
Reconciliation**

Client
Fells Point Corner Theatre

Designer/Typographer
Paul Sahre

Poster
Fish Head Soup

Client
ACT Theatre

Firm
Modern Dog

Art Director/Designer/
Illustrator/Typographer
Robynne Raye

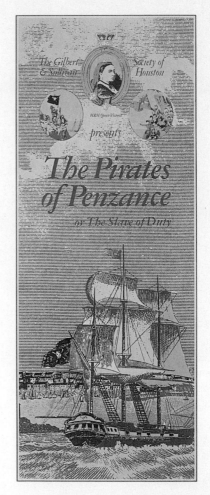

Poster
Pirates of Penzance

Client
**Gilbert & Sullivan,
Society of Houston**

Firm
Joseph Rattan Design

Art Director/Designer/
Illustrator
Joe Rattan

Poster
Heartbreak House

Client
**Seattle Repertory
Theatre**

Firm
Modern Dog

Art Director/Designer/
Illustrator/Typographer
Vittorio Costarella

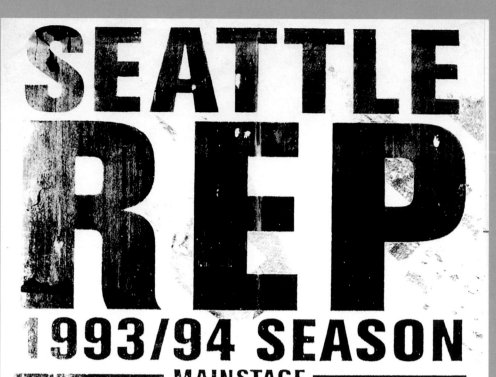

SEATTLE REP

1993/94 SEASON

— MAINSTAGE —

SIX DEGREES OF SEPARATION

HARVEY
OLEANNA

PERICLES, PRINCE OF TYR

A FLAW IN THE OINTMEN

HOLIDAY HEAR

— STAGE 2 —

NORTHEAST LOCAL
...LOVE, LANGSTON

SILENCE, CUNNING, EXILE

443-2222

Poster
**Seattle Repertory
1993-94 Season**

Client
**Seattle Repertory
Theatre**

Firm
Modern Dog

Art Director
Michael Strassburger

Designers
**Michael Strassburger
Robynne Raye**

Typographer
Robynne Raye

Film

Hollywood may be Dreamland, U.S.A., but in the realm of graphic design it can be hell on earth. The egos that heat up Hollywood on a daily basis contribute to the paucity of good advertising and promotional design. This is not, however, a new phenomenon but dates back to virtually the first posters and lobby cards ever designed for the motion picture industry. For rather than allow an artist to imaginatively interpret a film's contents, producers believed that posters and advertisements should exaggerate as much as possible while staying literal to the show. Movie posters routinely captured key scenes which were romanticized and heroized through hyperrealistic renderings of the stars or characters. A film's title screamed across the image in large dimensional lettering as it would across the screen itself. And the names of the stars, director, and studio were almost as prominent as the title itself.

Little has changed, graphically speaking, in the decades since the golden days of the silver screen at least in terms of mainstream Hollywood. But conventions have changed with the advent of more independent and alternative film companies and production groups which have tossed off many of the tired conventions that constrained graphic innovation. Small companies whose films are distributed through alternative outlets are less inclined to adhere to the Hollywood billing practices, thus freeing more space on the poster or advertisement for an image. But image is not a priori a virtue. Many big images say very little. The measure of exemplary art and design is how well it interprets the film, and how successfully it contributes to its allure.

Designing for the movies is often the exception to the thesis that graphic design is an integral form of entertainment. Print design must serve a very practical role to inform and promote the primary entertainment—the movie. If in the process it provides a comic or aesthetic compliment to the product then that is a surprising, additional benefit. Even the graphic tie-ins to certain movies are only entertainment in so-far as they slavishly adhere to the film. In fact, virtually the only designed aspect of a movie that can be considered an integral entertainment is the movie title sequence.

The most entertaining of these titles are kineticized graphic designs that owe a debt to Saul Bass's adaptation of his own expressionistic advertising iconography to film. In the '50s Bass set the standard for translating otherwise static imagery into often abstract animated sequences; he was soon followed by a handful of other graphic designers and animation artists who used titles to introduce a film's narrative. The few superb film titles that are currently being produced are like mini-movies that wed graphic symbology to storytelling, not unlike contemporary videos and TV commercials in which text and image are kinetically integrated.

While graphics for the film industry are always subject to the vicissitudes of ego, budget, and public taste, during the 1990s the advent of multimedia formats have encouraged innovations. Though not always as fresh as other entertainment genres, film graphics cannot be ignored.

Poster
Cinema Mexicano

Clients
**Festival Latino Film
The New York Film Society**

Firm
Paul Davis Studio

Art Director/Designer
Paul Davis

Poster
The Kill-Off

Client
Cabriolet Films

Firm
**Thomas Starr &
Associates**

Art Directors
**Thomas Starr
Jennifer Schumacher**

Designer
Jennifer Washburn

Typographers
**Typecrafters
Black Ink**

Photographer
Thomas Starr

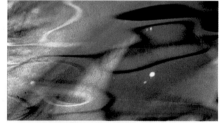

Film
Cape Fear

Client
**Martin Scorsese
Cappa Productions**

Firm
**Bass/Yager &
Associates**

Designers/Directors of
Live Action Footage
**Saul Bass
Elaine Bass**

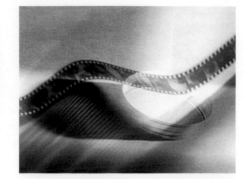

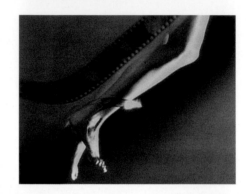

Film
**The AMC Film
Preservation Festival**

Client
**American Movie
Classics**

Firm
**Frankfurt
Balkind Partners**

Art Director
Kent Hunter

Designers
**Stephen Fabrizio
Gina Stone**

Photographer
Hans Neleman

Poster
Schindler's List

Client
Steven Spielberg
Amblin Entertainment

Firm
Bass/Yager &
Associates

Art Directors
Saul Bass
Art Goodman

Designer/Illustrator
Saul Bass

Film
Goodfellas

Client
Martin Scorsese
Cappa Productions

Firm
Bass/Yager &
Associates

Designers/Directors
Saul Bass
Elaine Bass

Poster
Filmex '85

Client
**Los Angeles
International Film
Exposition (FILMEX)**

Firm
**Bass/Yager &
Associates**

Art Directors
**Saul Bass
Art Goodman**

Designer
Saul Bass

Photographer
George Arakaki

Video Package
China and Sunsets

Client
00 Disks

Art Director/Designer/
Illustrator/Typographer
Robert Appleton

Photographer
Phill Niblock

Video Package
Four Video Translations

Client
00 Disks

Art Director/Designer/
Illustrator/Typographer
Robert Appleton

Photographer
John Katz

Poster
U.S. Film Festival

Client
Sundance Film Institute

Firm
Bass/Yager & Associates

Art Directors
Saul Bass
Art Goodman

Designer
Saul Bass

Photographer
George Arakaki

Poster
**Mill Valley Film
Festival 1994**

Client
**Mill Valley Film
Festival**

Firm
Michael Mabry Design

Art Director/Designer/
Illustrator
Michael Mabry

Media Kit
**Native American Film and
Media Celebration**

Client
**Association on American
Indian Affairs**

Firm
**Bernhardt Fudyma
Design Group**

Art Directors/Designers
**Iris A. Brown
Craig Bernhardt**

Logos
Turner Classic Movies

Client
Turner Entertainment

Firm
**Charles S. Anderson
Design Company**

Art Director
Charles S. Anderson

Designers
**Charles S. Anderson
Paul Howalt**

Illustrators
**Charles S. Anderson
Paul Howalt
Jeanie Jenkins
Erik Johnson**

Film Title Sequence
The Age of Innocence

Client
**Martin Scorsese
Cappa Productions**

Firm
**Bass/Yager &
Associates**

Designers/Directors
of Live Action Footage
**Saul Bass
Elaine Bass**

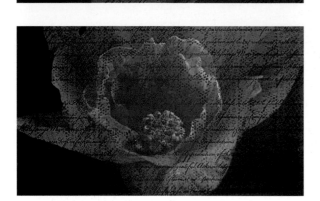

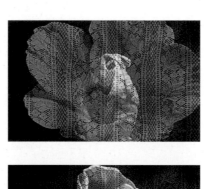

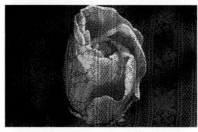

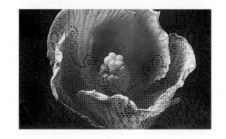

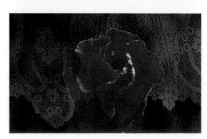

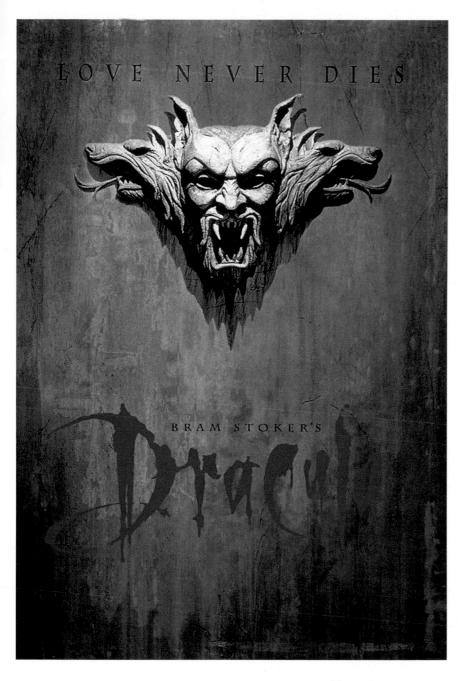

LOVE NEVER DIES

BRAM STOKER'S
Dracul

Poster
Bram Stoker's Dracula

Client
Columbia Pictures

Firm
Margo Chase Design

Art Director/Designer
Margo Chase

Model Maker
Jacqueline Perrault

Photographer
Sidney Cooper

Typographer
Nancy Ogami

Teaser Poster
Bram Stoker's Dracula

Client
Columbia Pictures

Firm
Margo Chase Design

Art Director/Designer
Margo Chase

Model Maker
Jacqueline Perrault

Photographer
Sidney Cooper

Typographer
Nancy Ogami

Beware

THANKSGIVING

Music

If music graphics be the fuel of sales, then design on. Born of marketing requisites to differentiate and identify musical styles and genres, the art and design applied to the record industry has evolved into the most imaginative entertainment graphics since Alex Steinweiss designed the first dedicated album cover in 1939. Record album covers—at least in their pre-compact disc 33⅓" format—became an indigenous American graphic design form, akin to the poster in Europe. By the mid 1960s record album design veered away from the late Modern manner of unadorned gothic typography and simple, impressionistic cover photographs towards a variety of raucous, crazy, and often weird graphics that typified the psychedelic era. The design of cool jazz recordings were at one time the most hotly experimental, but album art for rock and roll raised the temperature even higher. Owing debt to those designers who made music graphics sing during the '60s, the design for music today attracts the eye and toys with the senses.

From this era known for its memorable visual expression, perhaps the most indelible object d'art is the Beatles' Sgt. Pepper's Lonely Hearts Club Band, *the first "concept" album with what can be described as the first mature conceptual cover. Other "art" covers for music by the Beatles and leading rock groups had begun to push the boundaries, but Sgt. Pepper was not merely a concept—it was an icon of the age. It's hard to think of any other album that captured the imagination as much. It also set a standard for the extent to which designers could go to achieve visual pyrotechnics by using imagination and trickery.*

Although graphic design for music is not limited to record or CD packages—posters, flyers, print ads, T-shirts, and point-of-purchase displays offer a variety of distinctive formats—the medium continues to be the primary outlet for this kind of entertainment graphics. Today, mainstream and alternative record labels are the wellsprings of graphic innovation. The mainstream because relatively large budgets are available for lollapalooza extravaganzas, and the alternatives because their decidedly meager budgets force designers to develop unique ways of capturing the eye. Indeed the alternative labels offer the raw innovations that are ultimately appropriated by the larger companies.

With the virtual elimination of 33⅓" record covers contemporary music graphics are challenged by the lilliputian size of the CD package (except for multi-record collections, the wasteful "long box" has been prohibited since the early '90s). The compact image area tests the graphic designer's ability to adapt to visibility impaired surfaces. But the best designers are not only resilient, they have succeeded in transcending the constraints in both practical and entertaining ways. Moreover, the advent of the music video has inspired graphic designers to further expand the boundaries of appropriate imagery. Just as typography and illustration have been adopted by video directors, kinetic forms have been applied to print graphics. And owing to this confluence of multimedia, graphics for music continue to be the most experimental and entertaining of all.

CD Single
The Phantom Surfers

Client
Estrus Records

Designer
Art Chantry

goodbye

CD Package
Goodbye

Client
Atlas Records

Designer/Illustrator
Sheryl Lutz-Brown

CD Package
Sand Rubies

Client
Atlas Records

Designer/Illustrator
Sheryl Lutz-Brown

Magazine Spread
Monster Madness

Client
Rolling Stone

Art

Director/Designer
Fred Woodward

Photographer
Mark Seliger

Typographer
Eric Siry

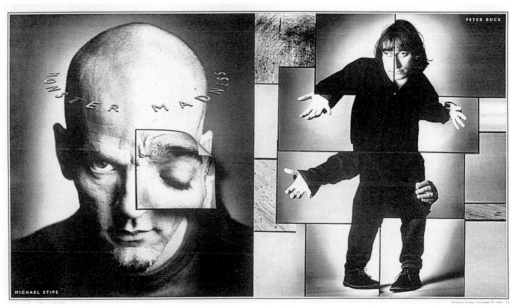

CD Box Set
Across the Great Divide

Client
Capitol Records

Art Directors
Tommy Steele
Andy Engel

Designer
Andy Engel

Typographers
Andy Engel
Bruce Licher

Photographer
Elliot Landy

Poster
October Project

Client/Firm
Sony Music Entertainment

Art Director
Nicky Lindeman

Photographer
Andrea Gentyl

Record Cover
Three Head Coats

Client
Super Electro Sound Recordings

Designer
Art Chantry

Magazine Spread
Birds on a Wire

Client
Rolling Stone

Art Director
Fred Woodward

Designer
Gail Anderson

Hunting
Two
Rachmaninoffs

Because I believe journalists should disclose their biases, I ask your permission to begin with a personal anecdote:

When I was 16 and living in a small California town, I began taking piano lessons with a young Russian woman from Odessa named Natasha. She had red hair and freckles and big green eyes, and although she put me on a strict diet of Bach two-part inventions and Haydn sonatas, I found that I was looking forward eagerly to my weekly lesson.

During my next summer vacation, I fell off my diet. On my own, I practiced Rachmaninoff's Prelude in G-sharp Minor—truly a piece of vintage Rachmaninoff, in which scintillating right-hand figurations accompany a haunting melody, full of longing, played by the left hand in the piano's expressive tenor register.

At my first lesson in the fall, with some trepidation, I tried my new piece out for Natasha. When I'd finished my stumbling rendition, she just stared at me for several seconds, her green eyes bigger than ever, then motioned for me to move over on the piano bench. Without a word, she sat next to me and played the entire prelude, pouring into it all her feelings for the faraway country of her birth, and some other emotions that, at that age, I was just starting to find out about. I was acutely aware, not just of the warmth of her playing, but of the warmth of her on the bench next to me.

After bringing the prelude to its pianissimo close, Natasha was silent for a few moments. Then she turned to me, smiled, and said, "You should study this piece."

So I must warn you, I am not objective about Rachmaninoff. But then, I know hardly anyone who is. The situation is not as polarized as it was twenty or thirty years ago, when the only "politically correct" way to compose was with the twelve-tone method. Then the wise heads of academia considered Rachmaninoff—who was born in 1873 and died in 1943—to be some sort of Victorian-Czarist brontosaurus who had lumbered by accident into the era of Schoenberg and Stravinsky. "His music...consists in essence mainly of artificial and gushing tunes accompanied by a variety of figures derived from arpeggios," wrote the British critic Eric Blom in the 1954 edition of *Grove's Dictionary*, the bible of music scholarship. "The enormous popular success some few of Rachmaninoff's works had in his lifetime is not likely to last." The effect of such scorn was to turn this composer's music into a guilty pleasure for everybody else, who knew that Rachmaninoff (more even than Chopin, Liszt, or Tchaikovsky, all of whom influenced his music) was the "romantic composer"—if by "romantic" you mean what it's like to sit on a moonlit beach on a summer night with someone you know very well, or expect to.

Today, nearly a half century after the composer's death, everybody can relax a little. At this distance, it doesn't seem quite so important whether the opulent Third Piano Concerto was composed in 1860, 1880, or (the actual date) 1909, just four years before Stravinsky's *The Rite of Spring*. Sensual scor-

After bringing

the prelude to its

pianissimo close,

Natasha was

silent for a few

moments. Then

she turned to me,

smiled, and said,

"You should

study this piece."

By David Wright

Magazine Spread
**Hunting Two
Rachmaninoffs**

Client
**Overture/Baltimore
Symphony Orchestra**

Firm
Carla Frank Design

Art Director/Designer
Carla Frank

Illustration
The Granger Collection

BOB
DYLAN
the bootleg series
volumes 1-3
[rare & unreleased]
1961-1991

CD Box Set
Bob Dylan

Client/Firm
Sony Music Entertainment

Art Directors
Nicky Lindeman
Chris Austopchuk

Poster
Shoukichi Kina

Client
Luaka Bop Records

Firm
Alexander Isley Design

Art Director
Alexander Isley

Designer/Illustrator
David Albertson

Poster
Social Graces

Client
Emigre Music

Firm
Emigre

Designer
Barry Deck

CD Cover
Play with Toys

Client
Emigre Music

Firm
Emigre

Designer/Photographer
Rudy VanderLans

Words and music written and recorded by JAMES TOWNING
"Seth Sez" written by SHAWN WOLFE. "James T. Kafka" co-written by SHAWN WOLFE and
MIKE WASHER. "James T. Kafka" was originally recorded by JOE KAFKA on the "Pretty Cold"
cassette. Strumming on "Citizen" and "James T. Kafka" and some drums on "Skullcracker" by RICH
LILLASH. Some words in "Citizen" and "James T. Kafka" were written by Dave Butler. Some voices in "Seth Sez" are from
Diane, Shawn, Carolyn, Dave & Amy. Artwork on "Citizen" page from a painting by Diane Perduk.
Digital mastering by Northeastern Digital Recording, Southborough, Massachusetts.
℗ and ©1991 EMIGRE MUSIC. All rights reserved. Printed in the USA.
Write to FACT TWENTYTWO, c/o EMIGRE MUSIC, 48 Shattuck Square, #175, Berkeley, California 94704

53:47

1. James T. Kafka
2. Emanation Feel
3. Immortal Earache
4. Electrical Storm
5. Tragedy
6. Seth Sez
7. Citizen
8. Collapse
9. Skullcracker
10. Watching Children Sleep
11. Douglas Rain
12. Closing

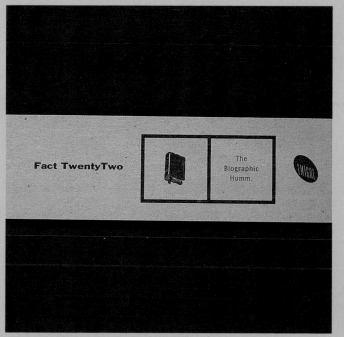

Fact TwentyTwo   The Biographic Humm.   EMIGRE

CD Package
The Biographic Humm

Client
Emigre Music

Firm
Emigre

Designer
Rudy VanderLans

Illustrator
James Towning

Poster
El Modio

Client/Firm
Atlantic Records

Art Director/Designer
Frank Gargiulo

Photographer
Amy Guip

Sales Display
His Boy Elroy

Client/Firm
Sony Music Entertainment

Art Director
Nicky Lindeman

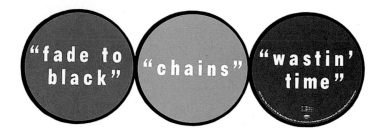

CD Booklet
Moonmaids In My Garden

Client
Ubu Records

Firm
The Design Group

Art Direction/Design
Stefan Sagmeister
Leo Burnett Design Group

Illustrators/Typographers
Stefan Sagmeister
Mike Chan

Photographers
Beni Blaser
Bela Borsodi
Hanson Fork

Media Kit
Volume/Vibe

Client
Time Inc. Ventures

Firm
Doublespace

Art Directors
Jane Kosstrin
Monica Halpert

Designers
Wanda Geismar
Jamie Oliveri

>Icons like
Chuck D,
Run DMC,
Queen Latifah,
Michael Jordan,
Fab 5 Freddy.
New names like
Dream Warriors,
PM Dawn,
Ce Ce Peniston,
Earnest Dickerson,
Marky Mark.
And those
whose work has
contributed to
the fabric
of the culture:
The Jackson Family,
Spike Lee,
Nile Rodgers,
Teena Marie,
Eddie Murphy,
Arsenio Hall,
Deborah Harry,
Afrika Bambaata,
Sandra Bernhard,
Aerosmith.

Mobile
C + C Music Factory

Client/Firm
Sony Music Entertainment

Art Director
Nicky Lindeman

CD Cover
**It Cannot be Exhausted
by Use**

Client
Larry Ankrum

Firm
McCall Pengra Design

Designer/Typographer
Karen McCall-Pengra

Poster
Dinamik

Clients
**Vladimir Kuzman
Dinamik**

Firm
Bennett Peji Design

Art Director/Designer/
Illustrator/Typographer
Bennett Peji

Photographer
Tamara Krupchak

Poster
Sin

Client
Sin

Designer
Art Chantry

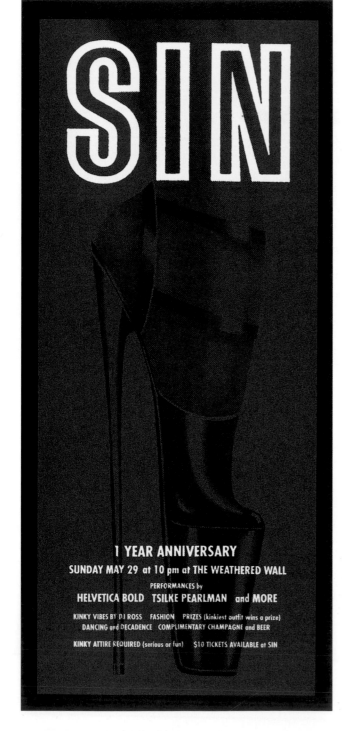

CD Single
The Beguiled

Client
Estrus Records

Designer
Art Chantry

CD/Package
Megadeth

Client
Capitol Records

Art Directors
Hugh Syme
Tommy Steele

Designer
Hugh Syme

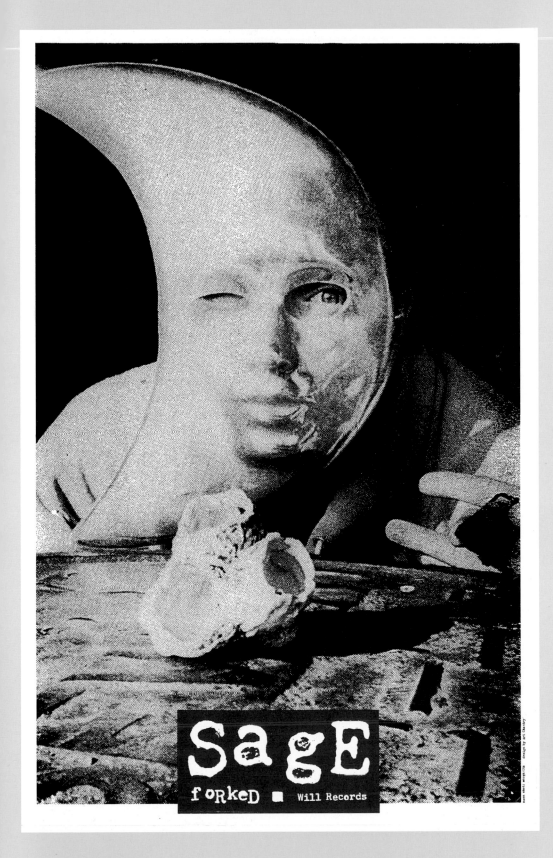

Poster
Forked

Client
Will Records

Designer
Art Chantry

Photographer
Margarita

Media Kit
More Protein

Client
Charisma Records

Firm
Red Herring Design

Designer
Carol Bobolts

Typographer
JCH

Magazine Page
Miles Davis

Client
Rolling Stone

Art Director
Fred Woodward

Illustrator
Philip Burke

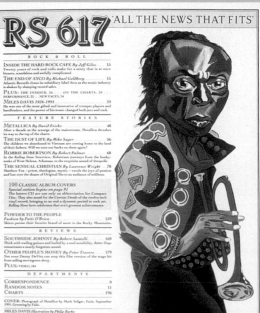

Record Cover
Treepeople

Client
C/Z Records

Designer
Art Chantry

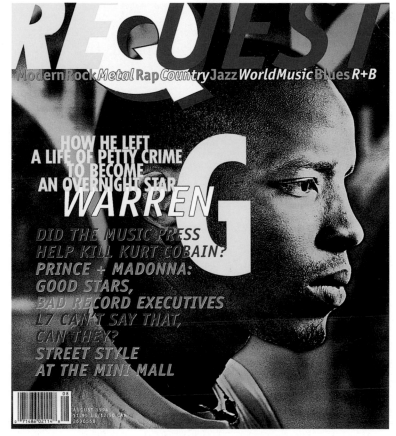

Magazine Cover
Request

Art Director
Scott Anderson

Designer
P. Scott Makela

Photographer
Michael Llewellyn

Logo
NPR

Client
National Public Radio

Firm
Chermayeff & Geismar Inc.

Design Director/Designer
Steff Geissbuhler

Poster
New Music America

Client
Brooklyn Academy of Music

Firm
Alexander Isley Design

Art Director
Alexander Isley

Designer
Alexander Knowlton

CD Package
Monster

Client/Firm
Warner Bros. Records

Art Directors/Designers
Tom Recchion
Chris Bilheimer
Michael Stipe

Photographers
Chris Bilheimer
Christy Bush
Jem Cohen
Brook Dillon
Michael Meister
Michael Stipe

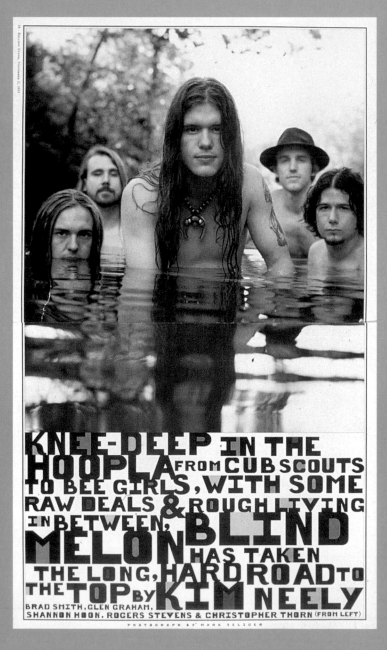

Magazine Page
Mouthing Off

Client
Rolling Stone

Art Director
Fred Woodward

Illustrator
David Cowles

Magazine Page
Blind Melon

Client
Rolling Stone

Art Director
Fred Woodward

Designer
Gail Anderson

Photographer
Mark Seliger

CD Box Set
Ray Charles Box Set

Client
Atlantic Records

Firms
Red Herring Design
Atlantic Records

Creative Director
Bob Defrin

Art Director/Designer
Carol Bobolts

Photography
Michael Ochs Archives
William Claxton
New York Public Library
Schomberg Center
Lee Friedlander
Bob Parent
Institute for Jazz
Studies, Rutgers

Typographer
JCH

Record Box Set
Cocktail Companion

Client
Estrus Records

Art Director/Designer/
Illustrator/Typographer
Edwin Fotheringham

THE ESTRUS **COCKTAIL** COMPANION

Tour Book
Madonna

Client
Maverick

Firm
Margo Chase Design

Art Director/Designer/
Typographer
Margo Chase

Background Illustrator
Jackie Tough

Photographer
Melodie McDaniel

Logo
Sweet & Low

Client
Sweet & Low

Firm
Phoenix Creative

Art Director/Designer/
Typographer
Eric Thoelke

Illustrator
Mike Neville

Record Cover
Teriyaki Asthma IX

Client
C/Z Records

Art Director/Designer/
Illustrator
Edwin Fotheringham

Painting
Gene Autry

Illustrator
Laura Levine

Photographer
Britt Bunkley

CD Covers
The Essential Series

Client
Verve Records

Firm
Polygram

Art Director/Designer
Alli Truch

Illustrator
Laura Levine

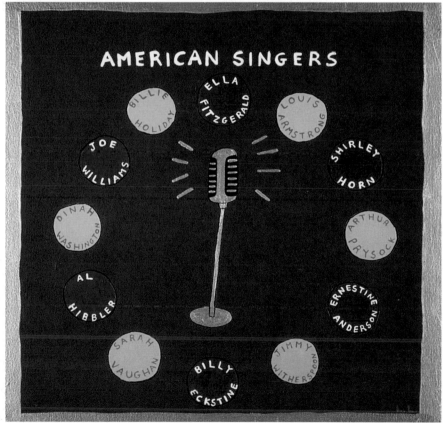

Poster
Juilliard IV, Flowers

Client
The Juilliard School

Firm
Milton Glaser Inc.

Art Director/Designer/
Illustrator
Milton Glaser

CD Package
**Automatic for the
People**

Client/Firm
Warner Bros. Records

Art Directors
Tom Recchion
Jim Ladwig
Michael Stipe
Jeff Gold

Designers
Tom Recchion
Michael Stipe

Photographer
Anton Corbijn

Poster
Juilliard II, Musician

Client
The Juilliard School

Firm
Milton Glaser Inc.

Art Director/Designer/
Illustrator
Milton Glaser

Magazine Page
Barbra

Client/Firm
US Magazine

Art Director
Richard Baker

Designer
Lisa Wagner

Illustrator
Hanoch Piven

Poster
Ringo Starr

Client/Firm
**Boelts Brothers Visual
Communication Association**

Art Directors/Designers
**Jackson Boelts
Eric Boelts**

Illustrator
Jackson Boelts

Guitar
Flower Guitar

Client
The Unconscious

Firm
Phoenix Creative

Art Director/Designer/
Illustrator
Eric Thoelke

Photographer
Stroube Photography

Bass
Reggae Bass

Client
The Unconscious

Firm
Phoenix Creative

Art Director/Designer/
Illustrator
Eric Thoelke

Photographer
Stroube Photography

Record Cover
4 On The Floor

Client
C/Z Records

Designer
Art Chantry

Record Cover
4 On The Floor

Client
C/Z Records

Designer
Art Chantry

Logos
Estrus Records

Client
Estrus Records

Designer
Art Chantry

CZ055

4 ON THE FLOOR

C/Z records

33RPM
TREEPEOPLE
Boiled Bird (3:44)
DIRT FISHERMEN
Soy Cheese (2:52)
GNOME
Crush (3:38)
ALCOHOL FUNNYCAR
Push (3:33)

1407 E. Madison #41
Seattle, WA 98122
℗ & © 1993. C/Z Records

Design by Art Chantry

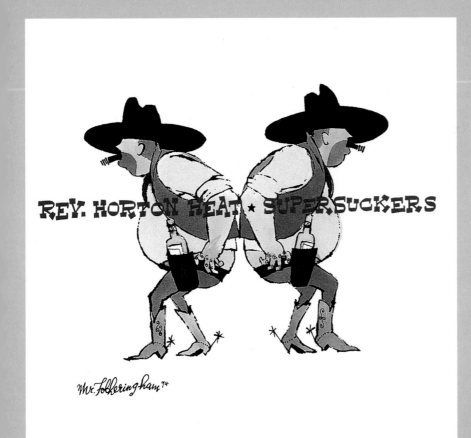

Record Cover
Supersuckers

Client/Firm
Sub Pop Records

Art Directors
Edwin Fotheringham
Jeff Kleinsmith

Designer
Jeff Kleinsmith

Illustrator
Edwin Fotheringham

Stationery
Chuckie Boy

Client
Chuckie Boy Records

Designer
Art Chantry

Poster
Boingo

Client/Firm
Warner Bros. Records

Art Director/Designer/
Typographer
Deborah Norcross

Photographer
Melodie McDaniel

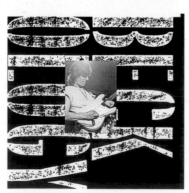

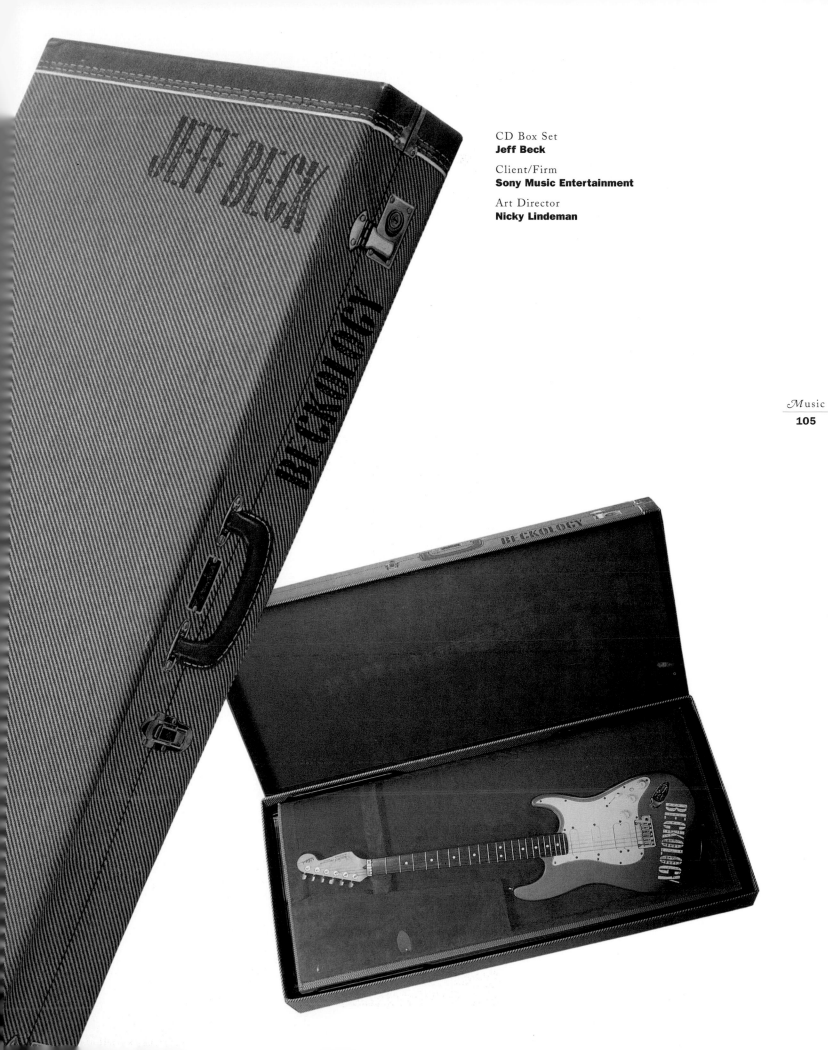

CD Box Set
Jeff Beck

Client/Firm
Sony Music Entertainment

Art Director
Nicky Lindeman

CD Package
Keri Leigh and the Blue Devils

Client
Amazing Records

Firms
Cumbie & Cohorts
Hungry Dog Studios

Art Director/Designer
James Ty Cumbie

Illustrators
Bob Tillery
Val Tillery

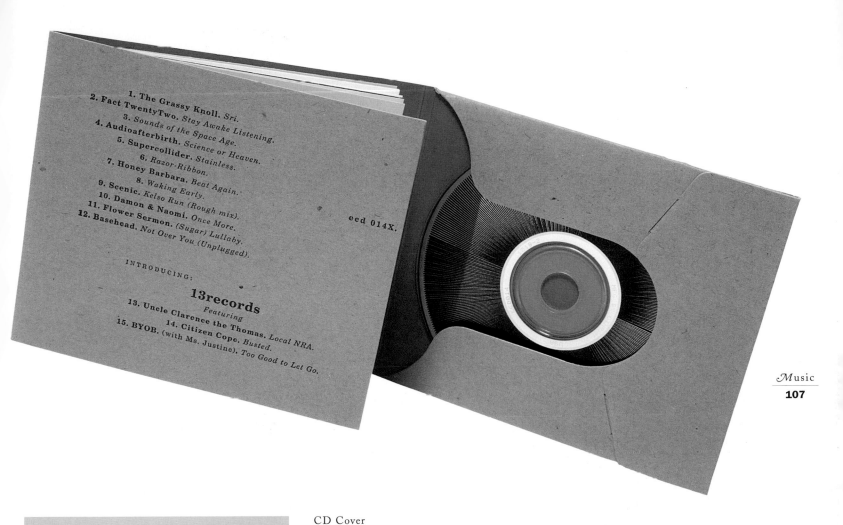

1. The Grassy Knoll. Sri.
2. Fact TwentyTwo. Stay Awake Listening.
3. Sounds of the Space Age.
4. Audioafterbirth. Science or Heaven.
5. Supercollider. Stainless.
6. Razor-Ribbon.
7. Honey Barbara. Beat Again.
8. Waking Early.
9. Scenic. Kelso Run (Rough mix).
10. Damon & Naomi. Once More.
11. Flower Sermon. (Sugar) Lullaby.
12. Basehead. Not Over You (Unplugged).

INTRODUCING:

13records
Featuring
13. Uncle Clarence the Thomas. Local NRA.
14. Citizen Cope. Busted.
15. BYOB. (with Ms. Justine). Too Good to Let Go.

ecd 014X.

The Emigre Music Sampler No. 2
(*Introducing: 13records*)

CD Cover
Emigre Music Sampler #2

Client
Emigre Music

Firm
Emigre

Designer
Rudy VanderLans

Photographer
Dan Olsen

Animation
**Everything in No
Particular Order**

Client
WXRT Radio Chicago

Firm/Creative Direction
Number Seventeen

Art Director
Emily Oberman

Director
**Emily Oberman
Scott Burns**

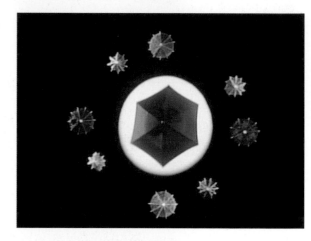

Magazine Spread
Nirvana

Client
Rolling Stone

Art Director
Fred Woodward

Designer
Debra Bishop

Illustrator
Terry Allen

Record/Package
The Angel in the House

Client
Elektra Records

Firms
Elektra Records
Red Herring Design

Art Director
Robin Lynch

Designer/Typographer
Carol Bobolts

Photographer
Melanie Acevedo

Poster
**Energy Work
and Power**

Client
Emigre Music

Firm
Emigre

Designers
**James Towning
Rudy VanderLans**

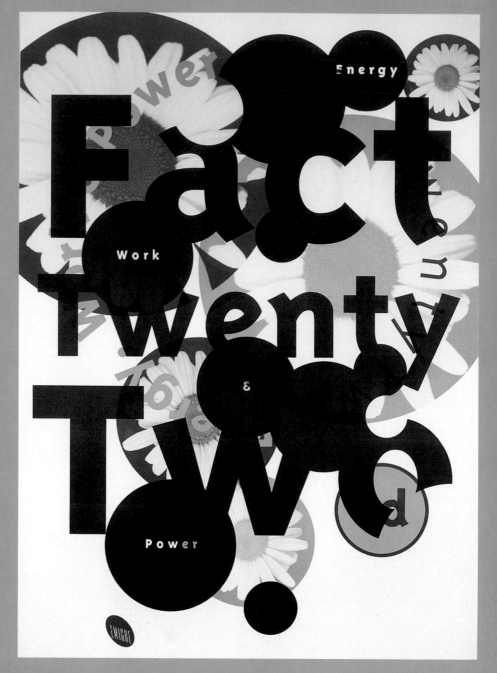

CD Box Set
**The Complete Ella
Fitzgerald Song Books**

Client
Verve Rocords

Designer
Chris Thompson

Illustrator
Jeffrey Fullvimari

CD/Package
Lava Hay

Client
Polydor

Art Director/Designer
Sheryl Lutz-Brown

Photographer
David Seltzer

CD Package
Sweetest Days

Client/Firm
Mercury Recods

Designer
Chris Thompson

Illustrator
Randahl McKissick

Cassette Cover
Street of Dreams

Client
PM

Firm
Phoenix Creative

Art Director/Designer/
Illustrator/Typographer
Eric Thoelke

Photographer
David Stradal

Magazine Cover
Overture

Client
**Overture/Baltimore
Symphony Orchestra**

Firm
Carla Frank Design

Art Director/Designer
Carla Frank

Illustrator
Mark Ryden

Logos

Firm
Joseph Rattan Design

Art Director
Joe Rattan

LLUMC Jazz

Client
**Lovers Lane United
Methodist Church**

Designer
Diana McKnight

Cyber

Client
Cyber Productions

Designers
**Joe Rattan
Greg Morgan**

WRR's Birthday Bash

Client
WRR 101.1 FM

Designer/Illustrator
Greg Morgan

Friends of WRR

Client
WRR 101.1 FM

Designer
Joe Rattan

REPRODUCTIVE
RIGHTS
COMPILATION

W ell over a year ago. with George Bush firmly in power. with the country's governing forces drifting further still to the right. and with personal freedoms and civil liberties under a ceaseless state of attack. I proposed the idea of compiling a record that would benefit a woman's right to choose. A lot has happened in the time that's elapsed between the conception and fruition of BORN TO CHOOSE—there's a new feline in office. and there's been a handful of similarly motivated compilations to hit the market—but don't for a second feel complacent. The two groups that this record benefits—NARAL (National Abortion Rights Action League) and WHAM! (Women's Health Action and Mobilization)—are fighting each and every day for the unalienable rights of quality health care for all and for a woman's right to choose. While a considerable pall has undeniably been lifted from all of our souls with the removal of George Bush. politics. as they say. makes for strange bedfellows. I wouldn't trust any politico as far as I could throw 'em. and we know what a problem Bill Clinton has with his weight.

   To all the artists. managers. record label personnel. and friends who selflessly gave of themselves to make this record possible. I'm eternally grateful. and what we've accomplished is great. indeed. And to all of you who have laid down your recession-era dollars on BORN TO CHOOSE. we thank you.   CRAIG MARKS

ZOE LEONARD seated anatomical model
GELATIN SILVER PRINT. 17" X 17". 1991-92
COURTESY PAULA COOPER GALLERY

Music
—————
114

CD Cover
Born to Choose

Client
Rykodisc

Firm
Emigre

Art Director
Rudy VanderLans

Designer
Gail Swanlund

312 337 fax > 3008
tel > 0008

320 WEST OHIO STREET
seventh floor
CHICAGO, ILLINOIS
60610

HINGE

Stationery/Business Card
Hinge

Client
Hinge

Firm/Typographer
Concrete

Designers
Jilly Simons
Susan Carlson

Poster
Deee-Lite

Client/Firm
Elektra Records

Designer
Carol Bobolts

Lettering
Taboo

Photographers
Michael Halsband
Adam Peipal

CD/Package
Fiesta Fatal

Client/Firm
Atlantic Records

Art Director/Designer/
Typographer
Frank Gargiulo

Photographer
Stan Gaz

CD Cover
You Won't See Me Cry

Client/Firm
Atlantic Records

Art Director/Designer/
Typographer
Frank Gargiulo

Photographer
Stan Gaz

Logos
Estrus

Client
Estrus Records

Designer
Art Chantry

Brochure
**Jazz at Lincoln Center
1993-94 Season**

Client
**Lincoln Center for the
Performing Arts, Inc.**

Art Director
Susan Panetta

Designer
Eric Van Den Brulle

Brochure
Jazz

Client
**Lincoln Center for the
Performing Arts, Inc.**

Art Director/Designer
Susan Panetta

Poster
Mozart 200

Client
**The Metropolitan Opera
Association**

Firm
Milton Glaser Inc.

Art Director/Designer/
Illustrator
Milton Glaser

Record Cover
Destroy All Astromen!

Client
Estrus Records

Designer
Art Chantry

CD Single
Monopoly Queen

Client
Sub Pop

Designer
Art Chantry

Photographer
Lisa Suckdog

Sharing the Joy of Music

Public school systems are strapped for money and slashing their offerings. Music and art instruction is disappearing from Baltimore children's lives. Where will tomorrow's audiences and musicians come from? Rosalyn M. Hamlett visits the BSO's new "Musical Explorations" program, in which musicians are going directly into area schools to ignite a passion for classical music in City and County youngsters.

Ruth Thornton Hawkins, a vocal-music teacher at Francis Scott Key Middle School in Baltimore, was nervous. She had 20 teenagers in her third-period music appreciation class and a special guest coming from the Baltimore Symphony, bassoonist Phillip Kolker, who had volunteered to play for her students.

The students were assembled in a second-floor classroom, dressed in baggy jeans, sneakers, and other paraphernalia of the hip-hop generation. They were restless and extremely adolescent. Ms. Hawkins worried that, in their exuberance, they might run roughshod over their guest.

Kolker is the principal bassoonist of the BSO and chairman of the woodwind department at the Peabody Conservatory. A tall, trim figure in a turtleneck sweater and blazer, he stood in front of the class moistening his reed between his lips and regarding the students through aviator glasses, looking perfectly at ease except for a slight tension in body language that suggested he desperately wished to please his audience. The students regarded him with a mixture of guarded curiosity and juvenile bravado. For them, it wasn't "cool" to show too much interest in a guy they had been told was going to play classical music.

Kolker hooked the strap to his bassoon around his neck, popped the mouthpiece into the crook of the instrument, and launched into a lilting theme which the students immediately recognized as the motive from Walt Disney's animation of *The Sorcerer's Apprentice*.

Suddenly the room became very quiet. Kolker continued, eyebrows arched, a hint of a smile seeming to play at the corners of his mouth as he adjusted his embouchure to the leaping intervals of the music.

Almost involuntarily the kids leaned forward in their chairs. Their faces were aglow as if all of their intense restlessness, frustration, and uncertainty were slowly draining from their bodies. It was an epiphany.

That these public school students, so often depicted in the media as distracted, alienated young people, could respond with such touching innocence to the magic of Paul Dukas' music might seem a minor miracle. In fact, their reaction was exactly what the creators of the Baltimore Symphony's Musical Explorations program had hoped would happen: that such exposure could be the vehicle for a life-affirming, transforming experience that would spark a passion for the kind of great music people the world over have loved for centuries.

Too often it has seemed easier for educators and politicians to write off children rather than imagine how to reach out to them on a level they can understand. Yet a tenuous balance is being struck between the area's elementary, middle, and high school students and the BSO through the outreach program that brought bassoonist Phillip Kolker to Francis Scott Key Middle School. Day after day, the Musical Explorations program, which was started last season and has grown significantly this year, is striking sparks of enthusiasm in children who never imagined themselves capable of enjoying "classical music." It is the hope of the program's creators that such sparks ultimately will both enrich the lives of Baltimore's youngsters and help stem the decline of arts education and appreciation in the metropolitan area.

From its beginning, the partnership has worked well. Young people who are excited by new sounds and accomplished artists eager to reach out to them are finding a natural bond. Lakisha Davis, an 11-year-old from Chinquapin Middle School, had never heard the orchestra in

ILLUSTRATION BY GARY BASEMAN

Magazine Spread
Sharing the Joy of Music

Client
Overture/Baltimore Symphony Orchestra

Firm
Carla Frank Design

Art Director/Designer
Carla Frank

Illustrator
Gary Baseman

the turbulent life and mysterious death of

Tchai-kovsky

DID A DESPAIRING TCHAIKOVSKY die by his own hand? or was he unlucky enough to be carried away by cholera just days after premiering what he believed to be his greatest symphony, the "pathétique?" as the centennial of his death rolls around on november 6, 1993—to be commemorated by BSO performances of the entire second act of *the nutcracker* ballet and that enigmatic last symphony—experts are still arguing the case for and against suicide. and as DAVID PATRICK STEARNS explains, the jury is still out on this tantalizing question.

icons by rip kastaris

Magazine Spread
Tchaikovsky

Client
**Overture/Baltimore
Symphony Orchestra**

Firm
Carla Frank Design

Art Director/Designer
Carla Frank

Illustrator
Rip Kastaris

Poster
Every Good Boy

Client
Emigre Music

Firm
Emigre

Designer
Rudy VanderLans

Illustrator
Liz Charman

Record Cover
Bali

Client
**Elektra/Nonesuch
Records**

Firm
Alexander Isley Design

Art Director
Alexander Isley

Designers
**Alexander Isley
Carrie Leeb**

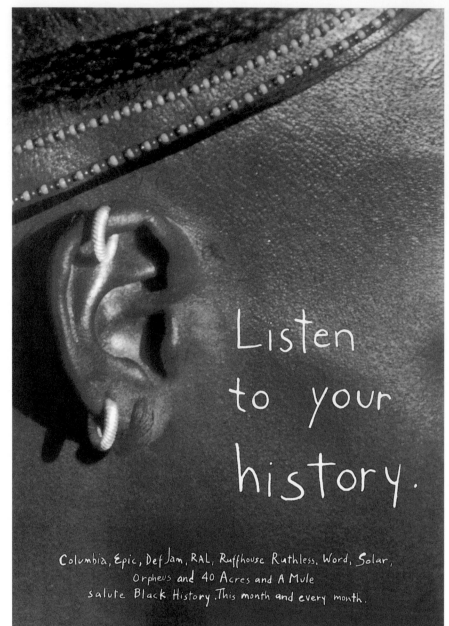

Poster
Listen To Your History

Client/Firm
Sony Music Entertainment

Art Director
Nicky Lindeman

Photographer
Angela Fisher

Sales Display
Grace

Client/Firm
Sony Music Entertainment

Art Director
Nicky Lindeman

Photographer
Merri Cyr

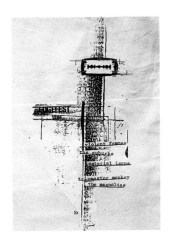

T-Shirt
Edgefest '94

Client
**Concerts for the
Environment**

Firm
**Charles S. Anderson
Design Company**

Art Director
Charles S. Anderson

Designers
**Charles S. Anderson
Joel Templin
Paul Howalt**

Poster
Inflatable Soule

Client
**The Reverand Bob
Jones/Barbeau**

Firm
Modern Dog

Designer/Illustrator/
Typographer
Robynne Raye

CD Box Set
**360 Degrees of
Black Music**

Client
**Polygram Group
Distribution**

Designer
Chris Thompson

Photographer
Paul Aressu

Identity
Sound of White Noise

Client
Elektra Records

Firms
**Elektra Records
BlackDog**

Art Director
Robin Lynch

Designer/Illustrator
Mark Fox

Logo
Unity 2

Client
Warner Bros. Records

Firms
**Warner Bros. Records
BlackDog**

Art Director
Mary Ann Dibs

Designer/Illustrator
Mark Fox

Logo
No Fake Tapes!

Client
Warner Elektra Atlantic

Firms
**Warner Bros. Records
BlackDog**

Art Director
John Bade

Designers
**Mark Fox
John Bade**

Illustrator
Mark Fox

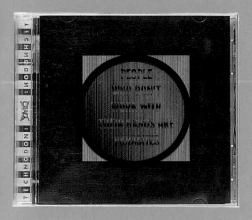

Record Cover
YMO Technodon

Client
Toshiba Emi

Firms
M + Co.
Sagmeister Inc.

Art Director/Designer/
Typographer
Stefan Sagmeister

Illustrator
Eric Zim

Photographer
Ed Lachman

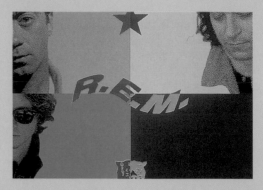

Interactive Disc
Monster

Client/Firm
Warner Bros. Records

Art Directors/Designers
Cecil Juanarena
Tom Recchion

Interactive Disc
Without a Sound

Client/Firm
Warner Bros. Records

Art Director
Dirk Walter

Designer
Cecil Juanarena

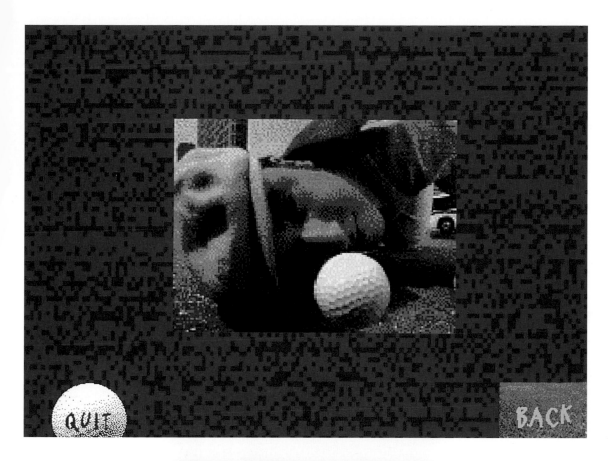

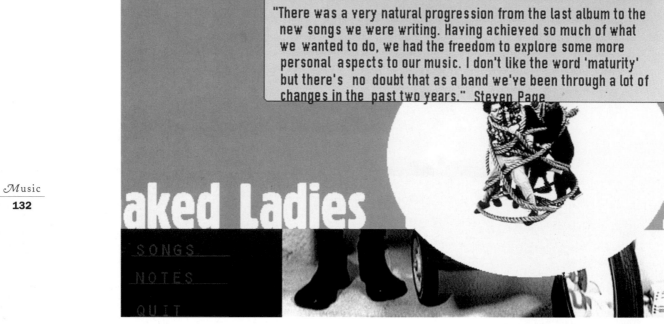

"There was a very natural progression from the last album to the new songs we were writing. Having achieved so much of what we wanted to do, we had the freedom to explore some more personal aspects to our music. I don't like the word 'maturity' but there's no doubt that as a band we've been through a lot of changes in the past two years." Steven Page

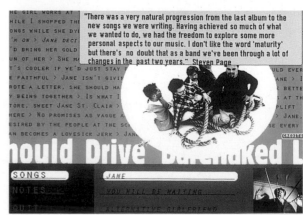

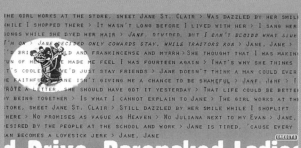

THE GIRL WORKS AT THE STORE, SWEET JANE ST. CLAIR > WAS DAZZLED BY HER SMILE
WHILE I SHOPPED THERE > IT WASN'T LONG BEFORE I LIVED WITH HER > I SANG HER
SONGS WHILE SHE DYED HER HAIR > JANE, DIVIDED, BUT I CAN'T DECIDE WHAT SIDE
I'M ON > JANE DECIDED ONLY COWARDS STAY, WHILE TRAITORS RUN > JANE, JANE >
I'D BRING GOLD AND FRANKINCENSE AND MYRRH > SHE THOUGHT THAT I WAS MAKING
FUN OF HER > SHE MADE ME FEEL I WAS FOURTEEN AGAIN > THAT'S WHY SHE THINKS
IT'S COOLER WE'D JUST STAY FRIENDS > JANE DOESN'T THINK A MAN COULD EVER
BE FAITHFUL > JANE ISN'T GIVING ME A CHANCE TO BE SHAMEFUL > JANE, JANE > I
WROTE A LETTER, SHE SHOULD HAVE GOT IT YESTERDAY > THAT LIFE COULD BE BETTER
BY BEING TOGETHER > IS WHAT I CANNOT EXPLAIN TO JANE > THE GIRL WORKS AT THE
STORE, SWEET JANE ST. CLAIR > STILL DAZZLED BY HER SMILE WHILE I SHOPLIFT
THERE > NO PROMISES AS VAGUE AS HEAVEN > NO JULIANA NEXT TO MY EVAN > JANE,
DESIRED BY THE PEOPLE AT THE SCHOOL AND WORK > JANE IS TIRED, 'CAUSE EVERY
MAN BECOMES A LOVESICK JERK > JANE, JANE

d Drive Barenaked Ladies

SONGS   JANE

NOTES   YOU WILL BE WAITING

QUIT   ALTERNATIVE GIRLFRIEND

1 Jane 4:04
2 Intermittently 3:05
3 These Apples 3:10
4 You Will Be Waiting 3:45
5 A 4:20
6 Everything Old is New Again 4:13
7 Alternative Girlfriend 4:23
8 Am I The Only One 4:49
9 Little Tiny Song 1:02
10 Life, In A Nutshell 3:14
11 The Wrong Man Was Convicted 5:06
12 Great Provider 4:35

aybe You Should Drive

SONGS

NOTES

QUIT

CLICK ONCE MORE
TO QUIT THIS PROGRAM

Interactive Disc
Maybe You Should Drive

Client/Firm
Warner Bros. Records

Art Director
Jeri Heiden

Design
Post Tool Design

Typographer
Jeri Heiden

Photographer
Alastair Tahin

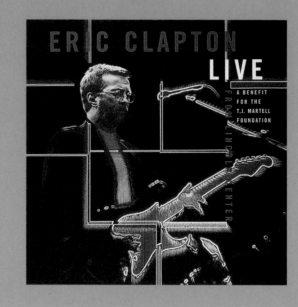

Book Cover/Spread
T.J. Martell Foundation

Client
T.J. Martell Foundation

Firm
**MTV Networks Creative
Services**

Art Director
Scott Wadler

Designers
**Scott Wadler
Tim Morse
Todd Barthelman
Karl Cantarella**

Illustrators
**Tim Morse
Karl Cantarella**

Photographer
Mark Malabrigo

ACCOMPLISHED.

COMPASSIONATE.

COMPLETE.

TOM, YOU'RE INCOMPARABLE.

BENEFACTOR

Elektra
Entertainment

Congratulations to Tom Freston.

WARNER & REPRISE
RECORDS

(And thanks to Eric for making this an even hotter ticket.)

BENEFACTOR

ZZZZZZZ...
WHAT? HE'S ON NOW?!

CD Package
Big Chief

Client
Tomato Records

Firm
Milton Glaser Inc.

Art Director/Designer/
Illustrator
Milton Glaser

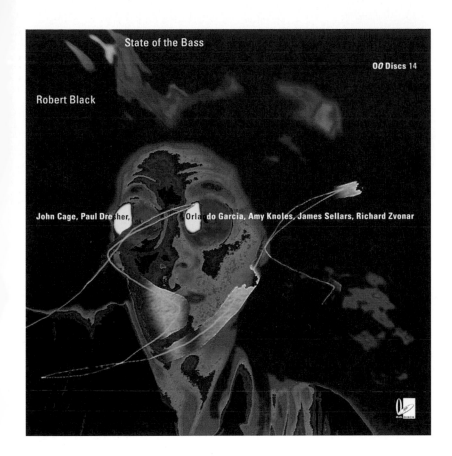

CD Package
State of the Bass

Client
00 Discs

Art Director/Designer/
Illustrator/Typographer
Robert Appleton

CD Package
Zeitgeist Plays Rzewski

Client
00 Discs

Art Director/Designer/
Illustrator/Typographer
Robert Appleton

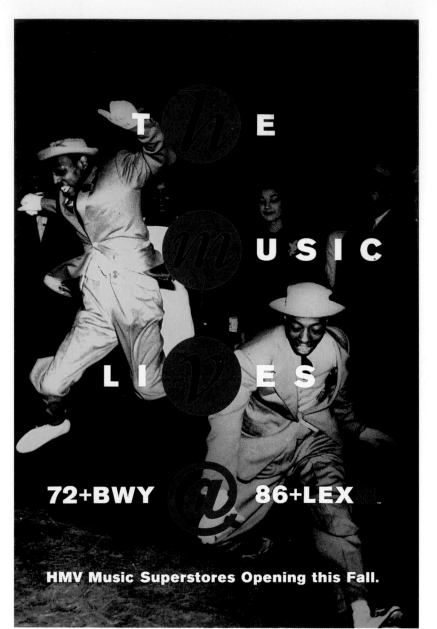

Poster
HMV New York Launch Campaign

Client
HMV Music Superstores

Firm
Frankfurt Balkind Partners

Art Director
Kent Hunter

Designer
Johan Vipper

Photographer
Herman Leonard

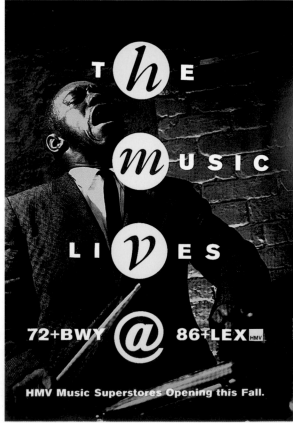

Sales Display
Blackfish

Client/Firm
Sony Music Entertainment

Art Director
Nicky Lindeman

CD Package
Blackfish

Client/Firm
Sony Music Entertainment

Art Directors
Nicky Lindeman
Chris Austopchuk

Photographer
Dana Tynan

Magazine Cover/Spread
Ray Gun Number 9

Client
Ray Gun

Firm
David Carson Design

Art Director/Designer
David Carson

Photographer
Lisa Spindler (cover)

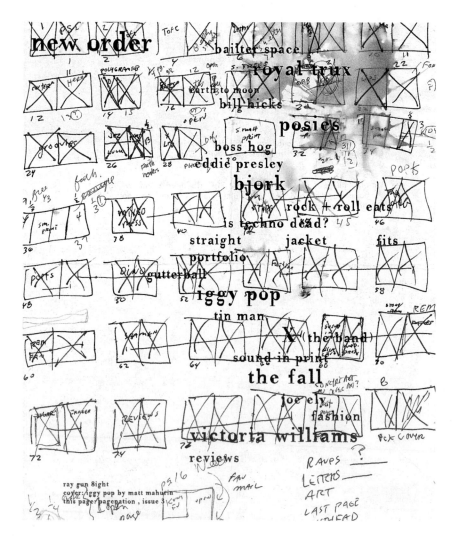

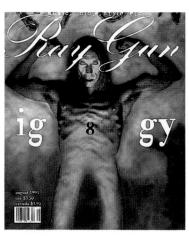

Magazine Cover/Page
Ray Gun Number 8

Client
Ray Gun

Firm
David Carson Design

Art Director/Designer
David Carson

Photographer
Matt Mahurin (cover)

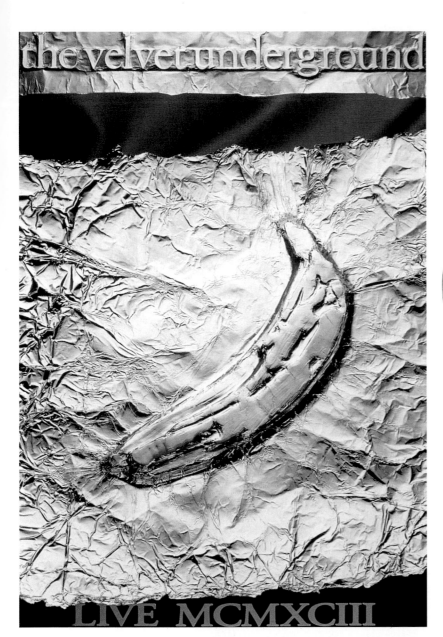

Poster/CD/Package
Live MCMXCIII

Client
**Sire Records/
Warner Bros. Records**

Firm
Justdesign

Art Directors
**Sylvia Reed
Spencer Drate**

Designers
**Sylvia Reed
Spencer Drate
Jütka Salavetz
Dennis Ascienzo**

Photographer
Ted Chin

Poster
Honey Barbara

Client
Emigre Music

Firm
Emigre

Designer
Rudy VanderLans

Illustrator
Edward Fella

Poster
Super Collider

Client
Emigre Music

Firm
Emigre

Designer
Rudy VanderLans

su per col li der

Magazine Spread
"And the winner is..."

Client
**Overture/Baltimore
Symphony Orchestra**

Firm
Carla Frank Design

Art Director/Designer
Carla Frank

Illustrator
Seth Jabon

"And the winner is..." The blaze of television lights. A deafening silence. Throats dry and palms wet, nervous contestants fidget on the sidelines. ∽ The Academy Awards? A beauty contest? A cookoff? ∽ No, it's just another music competition. Nobody knows how many of them exist around the world, but in the United States alone there are dozens at the young-professional level, and new ones seem to crop up every year. Competitions represent classical music's biggest growth industry, promising their winners riches and recitals, fame and professional management. ∽ But sometimes the fame amounts to little more than

Winning a medal at an important musical competition has become almost a required rite of passage for the pianist or string player who aspires to a major solo career. But in conversations with four upcoming BSO guest soloists—three of them victors in the competition wars—Scott Cantrell discovered some serious doubts as to whether competitions are the best way to pick the stars of the future.

Andy Warhol's 15 minutes, before the glitz-crazed promoters and public rush on to ogle the winner of the next contest. The winners, young and often naive, get devoured by agents

Poster
Dual

Client
Emigre Music

Firm
Emigre

Designer
Rudy VanderLans

CD Package
Ingenue

Client/Firm
Warner Bros. Records

Art Director
Jeri Heiden

Designers
Jeri Heiden
Greg Ross

Photographer
Glen Erler

CD/Package
**Transnational Speedway
League...Anthems, Anecdotes
and Undeniable Truths**

Client/Firm
Atlantic Records

Art Director/Designer/
Typographer
Frank Gargiulo

Photographer
Dan Winters

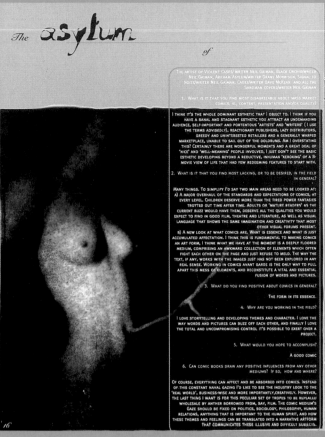

Magazine Cover/
Page/Spread
Blu r

Client
Blu r Magazine

Firm
Ride Design

Designer
Scott Clum

Illustrator
Dave McKean

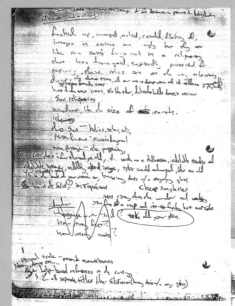

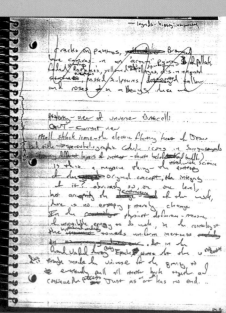

Magazine Cover/Page/Spread
Blu r

Client
Blu r

Firm
Ride Design

Designer
Scott Clum

Illustrators/Photographers
Doug Starn
Mike Starn

CONTENT

69

Television

Once there were three networks which dictated graphic conventions to all the smaller local and affiliate stations. Corporate aesthetics and mass-market design tropes pervaded the graphic landscape. Then this vast wasteland, as former FCC commissioner Newton Minow referred to TV in the 1950s, opened its borders to a veritable telecommunications paradise. With the introduction of cable the graphic standards applied to this, the most massive of all mass media, were formidably challenged. An industry that had been obsessed with "flying logos" and other slick electronic tricks was now faced with all new aesthetics born not of a need to appeal to the common denominator, but to strive for creative distinction in an increasingly crowded marketplace.

Not all network graphics were or are mediocre. The CBS "eye," designed in the late 1940s by William Golden, is still one of the most brilliant logos ever created. It not only continues unaltered to identify the network, but signifies the spirit of television itself. The NBC Peacock, designed in the late 1950s, taken off the air in the 1980s, and reprised in the 1990s, was a brilliant way to launch and identify this network's pioneering color programs. While NBC's corporate logo has changed for better and worse over the years, the Peacock has remained its most indelible iden-

tifier. And although ABC never adopted a symbol, it does have a resolutely modern logo, designed by Paul Rand in the 1960s, which despite all the digital manipulation applied to it, continues to be an unmistakable presence. In addition to these marks, over the almost 50 years of network television's history various on-air and print advertising graphics have earned top design awards. But in recent years network graphics have become increasingly pretentious in their overuse of technological conceits which have become associated with the paucity of imagination that corporate modernism hath wrought.

Enter MTV. Of all the cable options, MTV offered the most viable visual alternatives to the middle-aged network graphics. This pioneering rock and roll network did not only rely on music videos for its primary content, but was built on a unique graphically designed aesthetic. Whereas the network logos were classically Modern, MTV's was almost ad hoc—what one might call virtual graffiti. While the network on-air graphics were stylized and mannered, MTV's was raucous and experimental. VH-1, the music network of thirty-and forty-somethings, and Nickelodeon, the first children's network, also adopted distinctive visual personas; the former a slightly more mature, but no less exciting version of MTV, the latter an interpretation of a child's aesthetic without the usual clichés. These three cable networks became hothouses for graphic designers with license to test the limits of viewer and corporate perceptions. A plethora of video and print promotion materials not only forged their individual identities, but also signified the new age of new media.

In addition to these pioneers, special interest cable networks developed specialized identities. Lifetime, the women's network, launched on-air identifiers that collaged and juxtaposed women's faces next to a wide range of visual images and icons. The Comedy Channel, the first network devoted entirely to wit and humor, established a logo that parodied the network marks. And E! Entertainment, the 24-hour entertainment "authority," rejected all manner of slick, impersonal identifiers, for a repertoire of expressionistic and new wave symbols and marks which, when animated, project both a visually hip and sophisticated aura.

Although music remains the wellspring of creative entertainment graphics, television is inevitably more influential. The on-air and collateral print graphics for cable have had an impact on the networks, if only to keep from appearing tired and old. But as television turns more towards graphically literate multimedia designers for distinctive identities and promotions, what was once a depressed graphic medium will become a showcase.

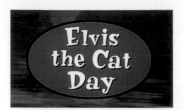

Animation
Nickdays "Elvis the Cat Day"

Client
Nickelodeon

Firm
Corey McPherson Nash

Art Director
Suzanne Archer

Designer
Tom Corey

Illustrator
Mary Anne Lloyd

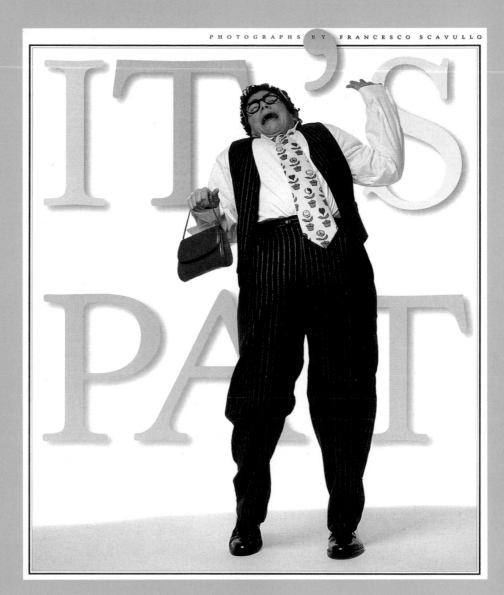

Magazine Page/Spread
It's Pat

Client
Rolling Stone

Art Director
Fred Woodward

Designer
Geraldine Hessler

Photographer
Francesco Scavullo

JULIA SWEENEY'S   gender-ben   ding character goes   to Hollywood,

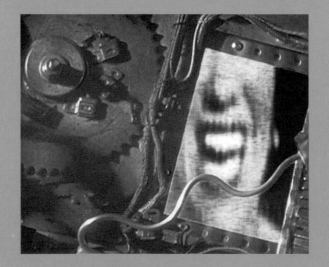

Video
**Short Attention Span
Theater**

Client
**HBO Downtown
Productions**

Firm
Corey McPherson Nash

Art Director
Tom Corey

Designer
Dale Graham

Animator
Mark Frizzell

TIMEWARNER

Logo
Time Warner

Client
Time Warner

Firm
Chermayeff & Geismar Inc.

Design Director/Designer
Steff Geissbuhler

Brochure
Star Gazer's Guide

Client
Comedy Central

Firms
MTV Networks Creative Services, Pull Time 3-D

Art Director/Designer
Scott Wadler

Illustrator
Steven Wacksman

3-D Artist
Gerald Marks

Photographer
Mark Malabrigo

Media Kit
ESPN2

Client
ESPN

Firms
Doublespace
PMCD

Art Directors
Jane Kosstrin
Monica Halpert

Designers
Catherine Williamson
Patrick McDonough

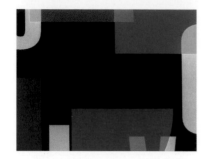

Animation
Telemundo Animation

Client
Telemundo Group

Firm
Chermayeff & Geismar Inc.

Design Director
Steff Geissbuhler

Designer
Robert Matza

Animation
Please Stand By

Client
VH-1

Firm
Number Seventeen

Art Director/Designer
Bonnie Siegler

Animation
Univision Animation

Client
Univision

Firm
Chermayeff & Geismar Inc.

Design Director
Steff Geissbuhler

Designer
Piera Grandesso

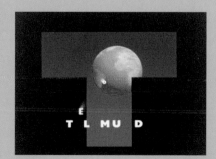

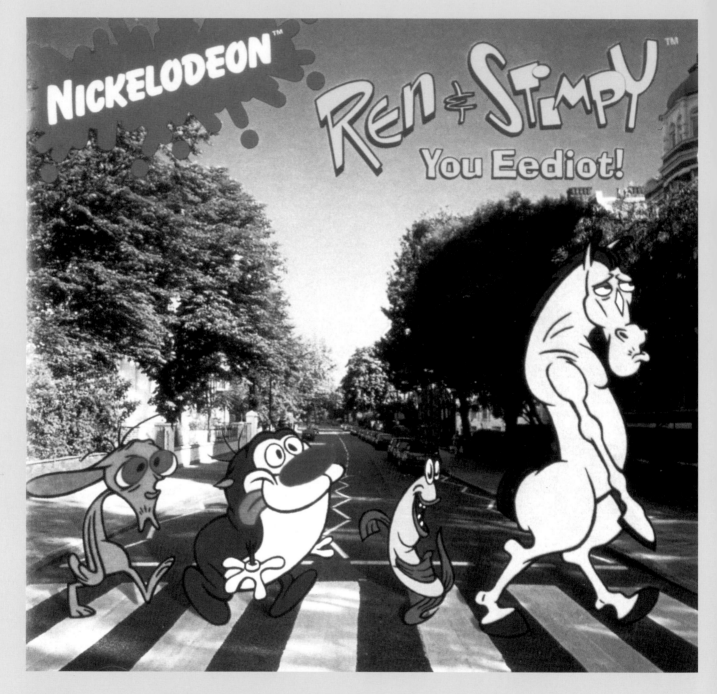

CD Package
You Eediot!

Client
Nickelodeon Sounds

Firm
Nickelodeon

Art Director
David Vogler

Designers
David Vogler
Peter Millen

Illustrator
George Bates

Photographers
Farquharson Murless
Mark Malabrigo

Photo Retouching
Jill Greenberg

Media Kit
E!

Client
**E! Entertainment
Television**

Firm
Vrontikis Design Office

Designer
Petrula Vrontikis

Illustrator
Huntley & Muir

Media Kit
E! Go Game

Client
**E! Entertainment
Television**

Firm
Vrontikis Design Office

Designer
Petrula Vrontikis

Video
Summer Top of the Hour

Client
MTV Networks

Firm
M + Co.

Art Director/Designer/
Director
Emily Oberman

Editor
Glenn Lazarro

Producer
Andy Jacobson

Creative Director
Tibor Kalman

Video Package
Are You Afraid of the Dark?

Client
Nickelodeon Video

Firm
Nickelodeon

Art Director
David Vogler

Designers
Sandie Goijburg
Nell Maguire

Photographer
Mark Malabrigo

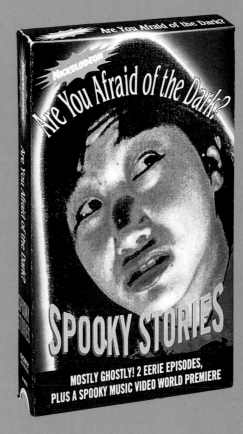

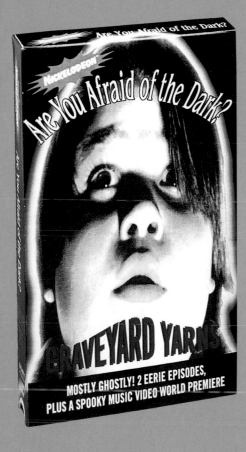

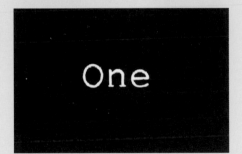

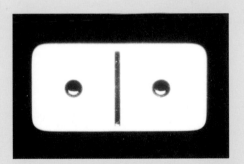

Animation
**Numerical Countdown
Video**

Client
**Fox Broadcasting
Company**

Firm
Morla Design

Art Director
Jennifer Morla

Designers
**Jennifer Morla
Craig Bailey**

Photographers
**Holly Stewart
Craig Bailey**

Video
fX Cake Shop

Client
20th Century Fox/fX

Firms
Cat & Crossbone
Corey McPherson Nash

Director
Graham Elliott

Producers
Mark D'Oliveira
Miriam Tendler

Creative Director
Tom Corey

Designer
Scott Nash

V H-1 IS

HAVING A BABY...

A MILLION DOLLAR

BABY CONTEST!

IT'S THE BIGGEST

PROMOTION EVER

FROM VH-1.

We're going to give away a million dollars—to one lucky baby (4 months to 2½ years old). We'll be announcing on-air the rules for the national contest, but it's really quite simple—viewers just send in a picture of their favorite baby to be eligible. The winning baby will be drawn at random from all the photos of babies we receive during a ten week promotion period that runs from March to May.

The good news for you is that VH-1 is ready to back this promotion with a million dollars of advertising and on-air promotion. We want you to get involved...it's worth a bundle.

Babies are big, especially for VH-1 viewers—our 25-49 year old viewers are busy having their own "baby boom". Those kids are a big part of their lives and we want to acknowledge that. When they see that their bundle of joy could win a bundle of money, they'll get involved in this easy-to-enter VH-1 national contest, sponsored by Downy Fabric Softener, and Gerber Products Co.

Brochure
VH-1 Million Dollar Baby

Client
VH-1

Firm
MTV Networks Creative Services

Art Directors
Jeffery Keyton
Scott Wadler

Designer
Scott Wadler

Photographer
Mark Malabrigo

Poster
Maigret II

Client
Mobil Mystery, Mobil Corp.

Firm
Paul Davis Studio

Art Director/Designer/
Illustrator
Paul Davis

Poster
Blue Boy

Client
**Mobil Masterpiece
Theatre**

Firm
Paul Davis Studio

Art Director/Designer/
Illustrator
Paul Davis

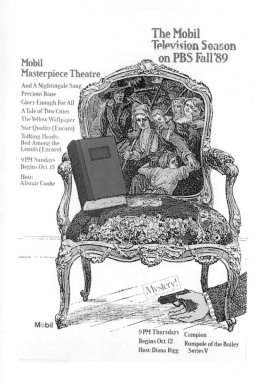

Poster
**Mobile Fall
Announcement 1989**

Client
Mobil Corp.

Firm
The Pushpin Group

Designer/Illustrator
Seymour Chwast

Typographer
Cardinal Type

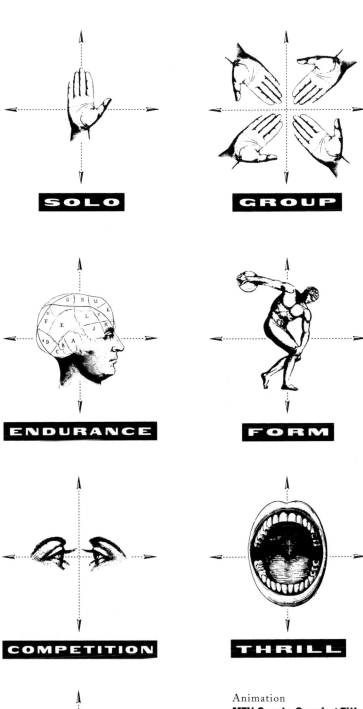

Animation
MTV Sports Opening Titles

Client
MTV Networks

Firm
Morla Design

Art Director
Jennifer Morla

Designers
**Jennifer Morla
Sharrie Brooks**

Typographer
Copy It

QUEENSryche

PRINCE

Royal BOX

SIRmix-a-lot

KOOLmoe dee

kidFROST

soundGARDEN

robertPLANT

flower BOX

guns n'ROSES

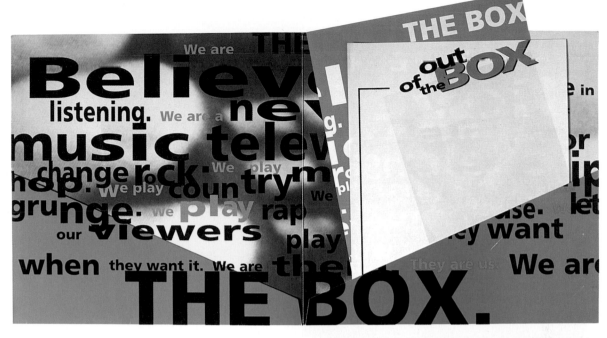

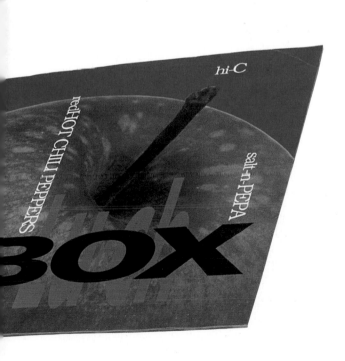

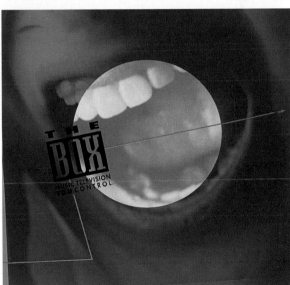

Media Kit
The Box: Repositioning

Client
Video Jukebox Network

Firm
Doublespace

Art Directors
Jane Kosstrin
Monica Halpert

Designer
Wanda Gelsmar

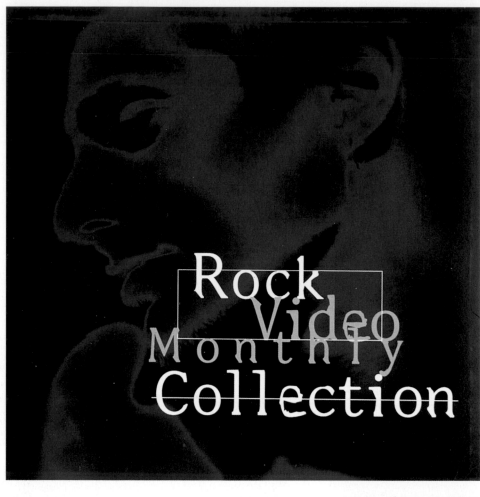

Media Kit
Rock Video Monthly

Client
Warner Music Enterprises

Firm
Doublespace

Art Director
Jane Kosstrin

Designer
Judith Kaelins

Typographer
Typogram

Video
**Reluctant Adults—
Laundry**

Client
VH-1

Art Director/Designer/
Director
Bonnie Siegler

Editor
Glenn Lazarro

Keeping 47,368,521 Americans
from becoming their parents

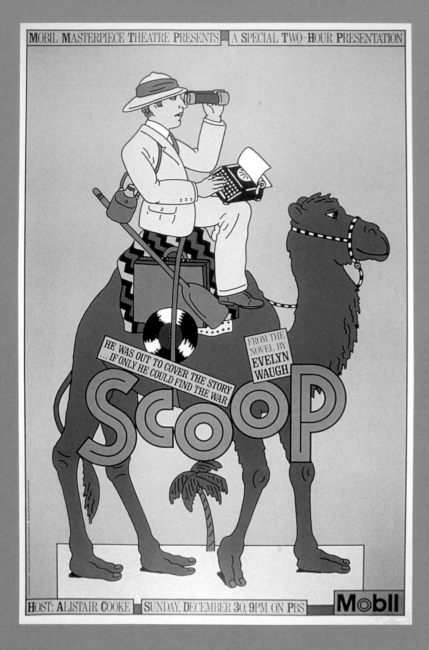

Poster
Scoop

Client
Mobil Corp.

Firm
The Pushpin Group

Designer/Illustrator
Seymour Chwast

Typographer
Cardinal Type

Poster
Poirot

Client
Mobil Corp.

Firm
The Pushpin Group

Designer/Illustrator
Seymour Chwast

Typographer
Cardinal Type

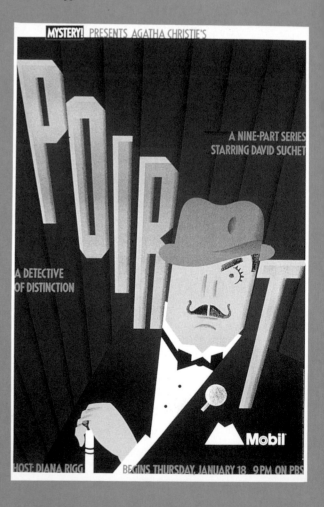

reason

six

We know how to reach *the ones with the most money.*

IT DOESN'T GET ANY
SIMPLER THAN THAT.

Brochure
Six

Client
Comedy Central

Firm
**MTV Networks Creative
Services**

Art Director
Scott Wadler

Designers
Scott Wadler
Jennifer Juliano

Illustrator
Scott Menchin

Magazine Page
Roseanne

Client/Firm
Entertainment Weekly

Art Director
Michael Grossman

Designer
Liz Betts

Illustrator
Hanoch Piven

Logo
Fox

Client
Fox Theaters

Firm
Chermayeff & Geismar Inc.

Design Director/Designer
Tom Geismar

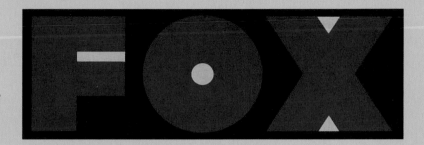

Magazine Spread
Seinfeld Rules

Client
Rolling Stone

Art Director/Designer
Fred Woodward

Photographer
Mark Seliger

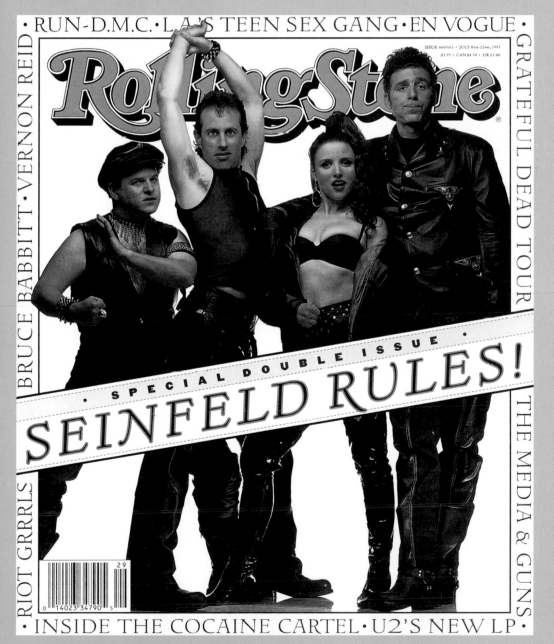

Special Thanks

The authors would like to thank the following people for their efforts in making this book possible:

DESIGN . . . .*Alex Isley*
Kristin Lilley

PRODUCERS . . . .*Mark Serchuck*
Penny Sibal

EDITORS . . . . *Susan Kapsis*
Deby Harding

EDITORIAL ASSISTANCE . . . .*Frank Zanone*
Alyson Heegan
Dorene Evans

TECHNICAL ASSISTANCE . . . .*Richard Liu*
Barbara Ann Cast

Appendix

Alexander Isley Design
580 Broadway, Suite 715
New York, New York 10012
Tel: (212) 941-7945
David Albertson
Alexander Isley
Alexander Knowlton
Carrie Leeb

Terry Allen
164 Daniel Lau Terrace
Staten Island, New York 10301
Tel: (718) 727-0723

Andresen Typographics
1500 Sansome, #100
San Francisco, California 94111
Tel: (415) 421-2900
Fax: (415) 421-5842

Robert Appleton
137 East 28th Street
New York, New York 10016
Tel: (212) 213-8544

Atlantic Records
75 Rockefeller Plaza
New York, New York 10019
Tel: (212) 275-2039
Fax: (212) 956-7289
Bob Defrin
Frank Gargiulo

Gary Baseman
443 12th Street, Apartment 2D
Brooklyn, New York 11215
Tel: (718) 499-9358

Bass/Yager & Associates
3039 Sunset Boulevard
Los Angeles, California 90028
Tel: (213) 466-9701
Fax: (213) 466-9700
George Arakaki
Elaine Bass
Saul Bass
Art Goodman

Beach Blanket Babylon
470 Columbus, #204
San Francisco, California 94133
Tel: (415) 421-4284
Fax: (415) 421-0518
Steve Silver

Bennett Peji Design
5145 Rebel Road
San Diego, California 92117
Tel: (619) 456-8071
Bennett Peji

**Bernhardt Fudyma
Design Group**
133 East 36th Street
New York, New York 10016
Tel: (212) 889-9337
Fax: (212) 889-8007
Craig Bernhardt
Iris A. Brown

Debra Bishop
309 Racetrack Road
Hoboken, New Jersey 07423
Tel: (201) 251-7660

BlackDog
239 Marin Street
San Rafael, California 94901
Tel: (415) 258-9663
Fax: (415) 258-9681
Mark Fox

**Boelts Brothers Visual
Communication Association**
345 East University Boulevard
Tucson, Arizona 85705
Tel: (602) 792-1026
Fax: (602) 792-9720
Eric Boelts
Jackson Boelts

Bela Borsodi
32 Thompson Street
New York, New York 10013
Tel: (212) 941-7875
Bela Borsodi

Philip Burke
1948 Juron Drive
Niagara Falls, New York 14304
(716) 297-0345

Capitol Records
1750 North Vine Street
Hollywood, California 90028
Tel: (213) 871-5156
Fax: (213) 461-1808
Tommy Steele

Carla Frank Design
4 Lexington Avenue, #4ML
New York, New York 10010
Tel: (212) 475-5840
Carla Frank

Cat & Crossbone
155 East 49th Street
New York, New York 10017
Tel: (212) 753-8226
Fax: (212) 826-8760
Graham Elliott

Art Chantry
Post Office Box 4069
Seattle, Washington 98104
Tel/Fax: (206) 441-3369

**Charles S. Anderson
Design Company**
30 North First Street, #400
Minneapolis, Minnesota 55401
Tel: (612) 339-5181
Fax: (612) 339-3283
Charles S. Anderson
Paul Howalt
Jeanie Jenkins
Erik Johnson
Joel Templin

Chermayeff & Geismar Inc.
15 East 26th Street
New York, New York 10010
Tel: (212) 532-4499
Fax: (212) 889-6515
Ivan Chermayeff
Tom Geismar
Steff Geissbuhler
Piera Grandesso
Robert Matza

Ted Chin
South East 19th Street, 4th Floor
New York, New York 10003
Tel: (212) 674-1871

Concrete®
633 South Plymouth Court
Chicago, Illinois 60605
Tel: (312) 427-3733
Fax: (312) 427-9053
Susan Carlson
Jilly Simons

Jim Coon
56 Arbor Street
Hartford, Connecticut 06106
Tel: (203) 236-5262
Fax: (203) 236-4863

Sidney Cooper
1427 East Fourth Street, #2
Los Angeles, California 90033
Tel: (213) 268-2627

Anton Corbijn
10 Poplar Mews
London, England W12 7JS

Corey McPherson Nash
9 Galen Street
Watertown, Massachusetts 02172
Tel: (617) 924-6050
Fax: (617) 923-0857
Suzanne Archer
Tom Corey
Mark D'Oliveira
Dale Graham
Scott Nash
Miriam Tendler

Cumbie & Cohorts
146 St. James Place
Brooklyn, New York 11238
Tel: (718) 399-2542
James Ty Cumbie

The Design Group
14 Tai Koo Wan Road, 6th Floor
Hong Kong
Tel: (852) 2 567-4333

Doublespace
170 Fifth Avenue
New York, New York 10010
Tel: (212) 366-1919
Fax: (212) 366-4645
Wanda Geismar
Monica Halpert
Judith Kuelins
Jane Kosstrin
Jamie Oliveri
Catherine Williamson

Drenttel Doyle Partners
1123 Broadway
New York, New York 10010
Tel: (212) 463-8787
Tom Kluepfel

Elektra Records
75 Rockefeller Plaza
New York, New York 10019
Tel: (212) 275-4000
Robin Lynch
Alli Truch

Emigre
4475 "D" Street
Sacramento, California 95819
Tel: (916) 451-4344
Fax: (916) 451-4351
Barry Deck
Gail Swanlund
James Towning
Rudy VanderLans

Entertainment Weekly
1675 Broadway
New York, New York 10019
Tel: (212) 522-1307
Fax: (212) 522-6104
Liz Betts
Michael Grossman

Glen Erler
400 South Hauser Boulevard
Los Angeles, California 90036
Tel: (213) 464-4481

Fahrenheit
169 West Newton Street
Boston, Massachusetts 02118
Tel: (617) 536-4482
Carolyn Montie
Paul Montie

Edwin Fotheringham
6049 Sycamore Northwest
Seattle, Washington 98107
Tel: (206) 706-9481

Frankfurt Balkind Partners
244 East 58th Street
New York, New York 10022
Tel: (212) 421-5888
Fax: (212) 759-9284
Stephen Fabrizio
Kent Hunter
Gina Stone
Johan Vipper

Mark Frizzell
Post Office Box 3176
Woburn, Massachusetts 01888
Tel: (617) 933-3150

Jeffrey Fullvimari
228 Avenue B
New York, New York 10009
Tel: (212) 460-8752

Stan Gaz
285 West Broadway, #270
New York, New York
Tel: (212) 334-7998

The Graphic Eye
1790 Fifth Street
Berkeley, California 94710
Tel: (510) 849-0560
Sue Ehnebuske

Steven Guarnaccia
31 Fairfield Street
Montclair, New Jersey 07042
Tel: (201) 746-9785
Fax: (201) 746-9786

Hungry Dog Studios
1361 Markan Court, #3
Atlanta, Georgia 30306
Tel: (404) 872-7496
Bob Tillery
Val Tillery

Huntley & Muir
14 Percy Street, Top Floor
London W1 P9FD
England

James McMullan Inc.
207 East 32nd Street
New York, New York 10016
Tel: (212) 689-5527
Fax: (212) 689-4522
James McMullan

JCH
352 Park Avenue South
New York, New York
Tel: (212) 532-4000

Joseph Rattan Design
4445 Travis, #104
Dallas, Texas 75205
Tel: (214) 520-3180
Fax: (214) 521-3180
Diana McKnight
Greg Morgan
Joe Rattan

Justdesign
160 Fifth Avenue, Suite 905
New York, New York 10010
Tel: (212) 620-4622
Fax: (212) 727-1322
Dennis Ascienzo
Spencer Drate
Sylvia Reed
Jütka Salavetz

Rip Kastaris
3301A South Jefferson Street
St. Louis, Missouri 63118
Tel: (314) 773-2600

Tamara Krupchak
1110 Torrey Pines, #13
La Jolla, California 92037
Tel: (619) 456-8071

Laura Levine
444 Broome Street
New York, New York 10013
Tel: (212) 431-4787

**Lincoln Center for the
Performing Arts, Inc.**
70 Lincoln Center Plaza, 9th Floor
New York, New York 10023
Tel: (212) 875-5384
Fax: (212) 875-5414
Susan Panetta

Mary Anne Lloyd
147 Wolcott Street
Portland, Maine 04102
Tel: (207) 773-4987
Fax: (207) 773-5362

Mark Ryden
541 Ramona Avenue
Sierra Madre, California 91024
(818) 303-3133

Sagmeister Inc.
222 West 14th Street
New York, New York 10011
Tel: (212) 647-1789
Fax: (212) 647-1788
    Stefan Sagmeister

Paul Sahre
1401 Belt Street
Baltimore, Maryland 21230
Tel: (410) 783-8764
Fax: (410) 727-7395

Francesco Scavullo
212 East 63rd Street
New York, New York
Tel: (212) 838-2450

Schumaker
466 Green Street
San Francisco, California 94133
Tel: (415) 398-1060
Fax: (415) 398-7295
    Ward Schumaker

Mark Seliger
96 A Grand Street
New York, New York
Tel: (212) 941-6548

Sony Music Entertainment
550 Madison Avenue, Room 2910
New York, New York 10022
Tel: (212) 833-5044
Fax: (212) 833-8501
    Chris Austopchuk
        Nicky Lindeman

David Stradal
1307 Washington
St. Louis, Missouri 63101
Tel: (314) 436-4996

Stroube Photography
3842 West Pine
St. Louis, Missouri 63108
Tel: (314) 533-6665

Sub Pop Records
1932 First Avenue, #1103
Seattle, Washington 98101
Tel: (206) 441-8441
    Jeff Kleinsmith

Alastair Tahin
7515 Beverly Boulevard
Los Angeles, California 90036
Tel: (213) 965-0899
Fax: (213) 965-0364

Thomas Starr & Associates
88 Cottage Street
New Haven, Connecticut 06511
Tel/Fax: (203) 865-2993
    Jennifer Schumacher
        Thomas Starr
        Jennifer Washburn

Eric Tucker
600 Flower Avenue, #5
Venice, California 90291
Tel: (310) 452-1905

Typogram
900 Broadway
New York, New York 10003
Tel: (212) 505-1640

US Magazine
1290 Sixth Avenue
New York, New York 10104
Tel: (212) 484-1787
Fax: (212) 767-8204
    Richard Baker
    Lisa Wagner

Eric Van Den Brulle
21 West 86th Street, #1602
New York, New York
Tel: (212) 721-2611

Victore Design Works
146 East 46th Street
New York, New York 10017
Tel: (212) 682-3734
Fax: (212) 682-2921
    James Victore

Visual Asylum
343 Fourth Avenue, #201
San Diego, California 92101
Tel: (619) 233-9633
Fax: (619) 233-9637
    Amy Levine
    MaeLin Levine

Vrontikis Design Office
2021 Pontius Avenue
Los Angeles, California 90025
Tel: (310) 478-4775
Fax: (310) 478-4685
    Petrula Vrontikis

Steven Wacksman
242 East Third Street, #9
New York, New York 10009
Tel: (212) 979-5667

Warner Bros. Records
3300 Warner Boulevard
Burbank, California 91505
Tel: (818) 953-3364
Fax: (818) 953-3232
    John Bade
        Chris Bilheimer
            Mary Ann Dibs
                Jeff Gold
                    Jeri Heiden
                        Cecil Juanarena
    Deborah Norcross
        Tom Recchion
            Michael Stipe
                Dirk Walter

Wexner Center for the
Arts/The Ohio State
University
North High Street at 15th Avenue
Columbus, Ohio 43210
Tel: (614) 292-4708
Fax: (614) 291-2955
    Alan Jazak
        Rich Rinsma

Dan Winters
6383 Bryn Mawr Drive
Hollywood, California 90068
Tel: (213) 957-5699

Eric Zim
333 West 22nd Street
New York, New York 10011
Tel: (212) 989-5147
Fax: (212) 989-5736

*I*ndex

The End